WHAT PEOPLE ARE SAYING ABOUT DR. KEVIN ELKO

"*The Sender* will touch your heart and change your life."

Andy Andrews, *New York Times* best-selling author of *The Traveler's Gift* and *The Noticer*

"Kevin is a tremendous teacher who helped the Dallas Cowboys train their mind, body, and soul to peak capacity. He truly has the power to inspire."

Bill Bates, former coach, All-Pro and Super Bowl Champion Dallas Cowboys

"Over my career at the University of Miami, I learned a lot of lessons from Kevin that helped lift myself and my teammates to a higher level."

Ken Dorsey, quarterbacks coach, Buffalo Bills; two-time Heisman Trophy finalist; former quarterback of 2001 University of Miami National Champions

"[Kevin Elko] has a unique way to touch people to become the kind of person they were meant to be. When I need a plan for growth, Kevin is my first call."

Andy Kalbaugh, Managing Director, Divisional President, National Sales and Consulting, LPL Financial Holdings

OTHER BOOKS BY DR. KEVIN ELKO

Nerves of Steel
The Pep Talk: A Football Story About the Business of Winning
True Greatness: Mastering the Inner Game of Business Success
Touchdown! Achieving Your Greatness on the Playing Field of Business and Life
The Sender: A Story About When Right Words Make All the Difference

Selected Audio Programs by Dr. Kevin Elko ....

"How to Have Your Best Year Ever!"
"Win on Purpose: Going From a Victim to a Victor"
"Boldness: Knowing What You Truly Desire and How to Go After It"
"The Power of Resiliency"
"Get Stuff Done!"
"Ownership: The Key to Greatness"
"So What Now What: A Mental Blueprint for Your Best Year Ever"
"Connection: The Secret to a Successful and Fulfilling Life"
"Maximum Performance Mindset: How to Take Your Athletic Performance
   to the Next Level"
"Keep the Main Thing the Main Thing: A Program on Leadership"
"To Do the Impossible, You Have to See the Invisible"

DVD Programs by Dr. Kevin Elko...

"Say It Out Loud!"
"How to Create a Winning Mindset"
"How to Be Truly Great"

Dr. Kevin Elko and Rev. Duane Thompson

BELIEVING
is seeing

TEN STEPS TO A MINDSET THAT WILL TRANSFORM YOUR DIRECTION AND YOUR LIFE

Whitman Publishing, LLC
PUBLISHING SINCE 1934
Whitman.com

Believing is Seeing

Ten Steps to a Mindset That Will Transform Your Direction and Your Life

© 2020 Whitman Publishing, LLC
1974 Chandalar Drive • Suite D • Pelham, AL 35124
ISBN: 0794848265
Printed in the United States

Correspondence concerning this book may be directed to Whitman Publishing, Attn: Believing is Seeing, at the address above.

The full catalog of Whitman Publishing books is online at www.Whitman.com.

CONTENTS

Coach Nick Saban on the field at a University of Alabama football game.

FOREWORD

D r. Kevin Elko and I collaborated on a concept during my last two seasons at Louisiana State University (2003 and 2004) and rekindled the project upon my arrival at the University of Alabama in 2007. The objective of our partnership was to develop a "Language of Winning"—both on and off the field—to teach to our student-athletes, coaches, and staff. It is a language that is repeatedly voiced and put into practice until it becomes an inherent part of our day-to-day activities. The goal for our student-athletes is to become fluent in these winning words, to themselves, to others in the program, and in their endeavors outside of football.

When asked what I ultimately want for our student-athletes, it is my wish to provide our players with every tool necessary to check all of the boxes in developing into men who will live happy, healthy lives; be productive and successful in whatever field they choose; and, subsequently, mentor and serve others. By instilling positive reinforcement and applying rational thinking in making sound decisions, we are well on our way to helping every student-athlete who chooses the University of Alabama football program become a well-rounded, principled man who can better provide for his family and community.

A key aspect of this language is having faith: believing in our coaches, believing in the training they receive, and believing in this incredible university. Nothing great can be achieved without faith. We have found that the probability of our student-athletes achieving success is significantly enhanced if they possess a trusting faith in themselves and in others. We, therefore, made it a priority that the trust and faith component is woven into the fabric of this language.

No doubt, there are challenges and, with social media so prevalent, we are now a click away from comparing ourselves to others and negatively deducing what it is we don't have or how we have been wronged. More often than not, the individuals who fall victim to this way of thinking lack faith and belief in themselves and their surroundings. When this happens, it's akin to a flu epidemic, and it can be contagious to others exposed to pessimistic/sky-is-falling behavior. Without a steady stream of reiterating core values, negativity and distrust can easily replace faith and trust. At Alabama, these challenges are tackled on a daily basis.

We view attitude adjustment much like we do a sore muscle. When a muscle is compromised, we work that muscle with care 24/7 and apply the appropriate therapy until completely healed. Likewise, strengthening a compromised state of mind is reinforced in team and position meetings, in the weight and training rooms, on the practice field, and with periodic visits by Dr. Kevin Elko. As head coach of the Alabama Crimson Tide, I am not just overseeing blocking, tackling, and play calling; I have a responsibility to ensure that the psychological welfare of our athletes is on par with their physical well-being—two fundamental elements necessary for reaching one's potential, and greatness.

An often-used phrase in Tuscaloosa is, "So What, Now What?", be it coming off a loss or winning a National Championship. The bottom line is, no matter what transpires, we believe we can always do better and will find good and opportunity in everything we undertake. This book is about just that: having an "I Believe" mindset and working toward and expecting good in your life. As you read Kevin Elko's book, you will see how many of his teachings and Language of Winning have impacted our program. Hopefully it will serve you well. Roll Tide!

Head Football Coach
Alabama Crimson Tide

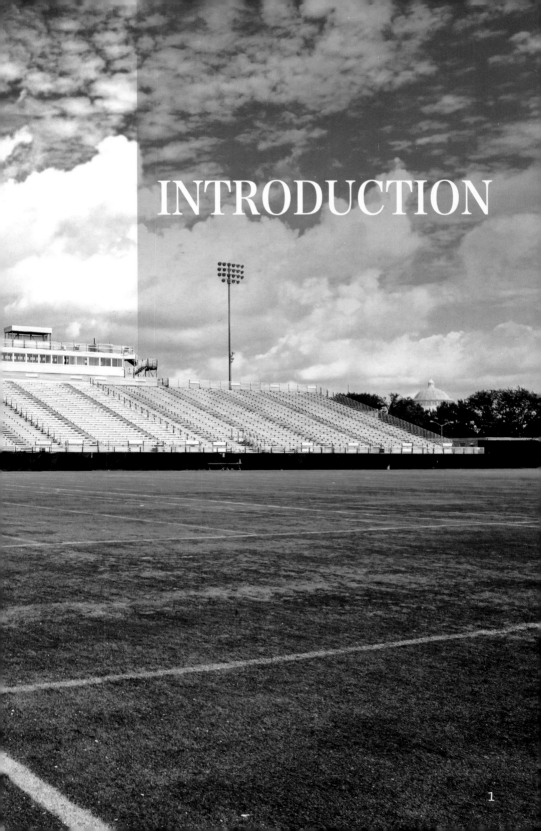

INTRODUCTION

The Pulaski Academy football team in Little Rock, Arkansas, has had a lot of success. They won eight state football titles between 2003 and 2019, including five out of the last six years. But what really stands out about this team is—they don't punt. I don't mean this figuratively, that they have a bias against punting, or they only punt when their backs are up against the wall, or in a long yardage situation. No. I mean this literally: they do not punt, they never punt, it doesn't matter where they are on the field, they always go for it, they don't even have a punter position on the team.

Think about the messages this sends to everyone on the Pulaski team:

1. We don't look back; we only look forward,
2. We are bold on every play, and
3. We believe we are going to make it every time.

And as a result, they often do.

Think too about the message this sends to Pulaski's opposing team: We are facing a football juggernaut of fearsome, determined players. They believe they will get the job done and get it done by running right over me!

Which team do you think is going to win the game most of the time?

Now the coach, Kevin Kelley, who is known for other unorthodox strategies as well (like relying on the onside kick and using laterals to keep the offensive play going), will tell you all about the computational analysis of data and statistics that pressured him to play this way. He will cite the Harvard study that says field position is overrated. He can show you with charts and graphs that going for it on fourth down even from your own five-yard line is better statistically in the long run than punting and giving your opponent the ball at the forty or fifty.

Still, people called it crazy—no one had ever played football like that before. Even Coach Kelley, who knew intellectually that it was the smarter way to play, had to convince himself to take the plunge and actually play like that, to believe enough in this method and in himself and in his team to really do it.

He finally came to the point where he told himself, "If I absolutely believe this, and the analytics that support it, then I don't feel like I am doing what I'm supposed to be doing as a football coach and giving our kids the best chance [unless I put this into practice]." Which is what he did.

The results speak for themselves.

This book is about getting rid of the punter in you who is always willing to play it safe on fourth down, and developing a radical belief mindset that will move your life forward.

Coach Kevin Kelley on the sidelines of a Pulaski Academy Bruins game.

I believe that, in any given situation, you know what you should be doing. You know, for example, that what you say to yourself, the words you speak into your mind and heart, are absolutely critical in creating a great life and significant future. You also know that having a vision for what you will become and how you will get there, having that picture in your mind and rehearsing it over and over mentally, will allow that vision to become your life. (These are the ideas we will encounter in our first two chapters.) Studies and research provide a high degree of certainty in this area. Proven life stories and anecdotes give you further evidence as well as motivation and inspiration. You can probably feel it intuitively in your core that it is true.

The only thing lacking is the answer to the question you must ask yourself: Do I really believe it, that what I say to myself will have an effect on my life and that my vision of my future will become my reality? Do I believe it enough to put it into practice?

Like Coach Kelley, if the evidence from the analytics and common-sense understanding and your own experience suggest that it is real and true, then the only way to give yourself the best chance possible in life is to believe in it wholeheartedly and go for it!

Sometimes, though, we have to believe in spite of what appears to be contrary evidence.

My next-door neighbor Lee Ford was hit by a car while he was walking across the street in downtown Pittsburgh. He was initially given one hour to live. Then the doctors updated his status, giving him one day to live. Then they updated it to one week to live. Then again, they said he was going to live but be blind and a quadriplegic. The final update stated that he will eventually be fine and achieve a 100 percent recovery.

I asked Lee how he was able to recuperate like that. He told me this was not the first time he'd received challenging news. His first wife ran off with his best friend. He later remarried and his first child from this marriage was diagnosed with Down Syndrome. He said the first thing he heard after being hit by the car was the doctors saying he was not going to make it. But he had been told that before—that there was no way to recover from certain things. He chose to believe everything in him that said he would make it. He had made it before, and he would do so again.

Sometimes, as I say, we have to believe in spite of the evidence.

Jim Wallis, who is working to help people overcome poverty and discrimination, has the best definition of the word "hope" I've ever come across. He says hope is "believing in spite of the evidence and then watching the evidence change." You can apply this to your individual life, just as my friend Lee Ford

Jim Wallis is a theologian and advocate for peace and overcoming poverty.

did. You can see the evidence of what your life is like right now, the circumstances that may be difficult, the situation that at times seems hopeless; you can hear what other people, like those doctors, are saying about your chances. And then you can believe, in spite of all that evidence, that the end result of your life will be so vastly different and better than what you are experiencing right now. You can put your belief into action today and tomorrow and every day, until you watch the evidence begin to change.

That is what this book is about: Creating the right attitude and dynamics in your life to give you the best chance at the most powerful and significant life possible.

To believe in what you tell yourself, to believe in the vision of what you can become, to believe in your own resilience over obstacles, to believe in your purpose, to believe in your past and your future, to believe in the impact you can have on the world, to believe in these and other things—that is the key to winning and thriving.

Like never punting on fourth down, it is rare. But you must be that rare person. It is believing, or failing to believe, that is key.

And it is your choice.

You are not a born winner or born loser. In so many ways, you are a born chooser. And greatness, I often tell people, isn't for the chosen few, but for the few who choose.

Most people are driven not by choices but by feelings. They see belief and faith, and even things like happiness and hopefulness, as feelings; you either feel these things or you don't. However, believing is not a feeling, it is a choice. If you don't choose, other things, usually things like fear and doubt and cynicism, will make the choice for you. You must come to see that so much of your life, almost everything, is a choice, your choice.

I have difficult and discouraging days like everyone, and at times heartbreaking and demoralizing events happen to me. What seem to come naturally are feelings that I want to quit or that I can't do this. I have to stop myself and say, "Today my feelings don't get a vote. I will choose faith and strength. Today I choose to believe." I see it every day in my own life and in the lives of others around me.

We must choose what we want our lives to be.

In 2003, I spoke to the Louisiana State University football team and another well-known college team in the same week. I don't always do this, but in this instance, I delivered the exact same message. Marcus Spears of LSU, who now

The LSU football stadium.

works for ESPN, wrote on the Internet immediately afterward that my speech was the best talk he had ever heard. Meanwhile, a player from the other team posted that he got nothing from it. Now, how is it that one team heard a message and said it was great and influenced the way they lived and played football, and another team heard the exact same message and said it was nothing? I think one group listened with belief and destiny in mind, and the other merely heard a bunch of words. One group chose to listen and get something out of it; the other didn't choose, but was simply an unwilling and uninterested part of an audience, and let cynicism choose them.

By the way, that year LSU won the national championship and the other team went 6-6. I don't want to be immodest here, but I did find this interesting.

So, you must enter every endeavor with belief. In fact, you must first choose to believe before you even begin. It sounds silly, but it is almost believing in belief. You have to believe that your belief will make a difference. Everywhere you look these days, faith and belief are missing. They have been replaced with hesitation and uncertainty and anxiety. And yet, to believe mobilizes and overcomes and motivates and creates an impact. Belief provides its own momentum.

It may seem crazy, it may never have been done before, in whatever field in which you are engaging. But whether you believe because the evidence is so compelling, or you believe in spite of the evidence, to believe is exactly what it will take to get there. It was Steve Jobs who once said, "Those who are crazy enough to think they can change the world usually do."

So, the question is not, "Are your thoughts and dreams too crazy?" The real question is, "Are they too sane?" Having faith in your crazy, outlandish dream might turn out to be what your whole life is about, and it may be just what the world needs right now!

1 THERMOMETER OR THERMOSTAT

Believe In What You Tell Yourself

Jacquelyn Mitchard was a journalist who was also trying to write her first novel. She was struggling like all first-time writers, thinking she would never make it, never finish, never get published, never be a real writer. In addition, her husband became seriously ill with cancer, and it was clear pretty quickly that he was not going to get better.

It was a truly awful time in her life, trying to care for her dying husband and their children, and trying to write.

One night, things just fell apart. She broke down and wailed inconsolably to her husband about how she couldn't take it anymore, she couldn't live without him, and how she was never going to be a writer.

And her husband, who had somehow managed to remain pretty calm throughout his illness, said to her very gently, "Listen, in two years' time, you'll be far from here. You will be a published novelist; you'll be a writer of merit. But you have to believe in it, like I believe in you."

After he died, she remembered those words; they penetrated into her mind and into her life, they influenced the decisions she made. She did things that others thought were incautious and risky: she took three weeks off from her job to go to an artists' foundation so she could write uninterrupted every day, and when she got a small advance on her book, she took an indefinite leave of absence in order to finish it.

She thought of her husband's words once more as she was making the final revisions to her novel. Life had been difficult at times, even impossible; often she was sure she would never make it, but here at last her book was finished and ready to be published. She didn't know it yet, but it would soon be a bestseller, selling over three million copies, and it would be the first selection ever by Oprah Winfrey for her Book Club; it would eventually be made into a movie.

The title of that first novel was *The Deep End of the Ocean*. As she was closing in on the final revisions one evening, she suddenly realized that it had been two years—to the day—since her husband had uttered those precious words: "You will be a writer of merit. But you have to believe in it, like I believe in you."

Jacquelyn Mitchard lived with those words, she allowed them to sink into her mind and heart. The words motivated her, compelled her to action, drove her to be bold and daring in what she thought she could do and accomplish.

Have you ever thought about how powerful words can be? Do you think words have power?

I know it's been said that, "Sticks and stones may break my bones, but words will never hurt me." Do you think anyone who ever said that really believed it? Words of ridicule and cruelty and hate can stay with you and penetrate deep into the core of who you are, crushing you more than sticks and stones ever could.

Likewise, words of encouragement and love and hope can stay with you and penetrate—and lift you up. Winston Churchill once said that sometimes words are more than just words; they are real, they are action, they create something and do something.

I heard someone in a speech once compare two great communicators in the ancient world, Cicero and Julius Caesar. It was said of Cicero, the incomparable Roman orator, that when he spoke, people would say how beautiful his words were and how eloquent he was, but when Caesar spoke, people were ready to march.

I think words have this tremendous power. The only question is: what kinds of words are we going to speak?

My co-author is a minister, and one day he received two voicemails within minutes of each other, with two very different messages. The first was from someone in the church who had just been to visit another church member, Hazel, who was in the hospital, and he wanted the minister to know that Hazel was not doing well at all, the doctor was not giving her much of a chance, the minister had better get over there pretty soon if he wanted to see her again, this could be the end of the line for Hazel!

Well, my co-author was ready to run out the door and get over to the hospital, until he listened to the second message. It was from another member of the church who had also been to visit Hazel, and this person said Hazel was doing well, she was looking good, and had a healthy appetite, it might take a little while, but the doctor said that she should make a full recovery. He still got over to the hospital that day to visit Hazel, but at a more leisurely pace.

It won't surprise you to learn that the first person was pretty pessimistic about everything; the sky was always falling, the glass always half—or even completely—empty. And it won't surprise you that the second person was almost always pretty upbeat, optimistic, and positive. Yet hearing those two messages with diametrically opposite views of the same person, the same condition, within minutes of each other just reinforces the basic truth that so much of life depends on our outlook, our attitude, and our words.

Perhaps the biggest question in this regard is: what outlook, what attitude, and *what words*, am I going to offer to the world, what words am I going to release into the life of another person? Words that are negative and cynical, that are cruel, that do damage? Or am I going to offer words of life and blessing, words that encourage and inspire, words of hope?

To get right to the most basic level of this, right into the heart of the matter: What words am I going to offer to myself? What words am I going to release into my own daily life, unleash into the very core of who I am? An article in the *Wall Street Journal* said depressed and anxious people speak differently than happy people. At the root of many depressed and anxious thoughts is constant talk about negative things, talk about what isn't going right and what they don't have. Happy people, on the other hand, talk on a more positive level; they talk about the good things and the great people they have in their lives and about their ideas and plans for what they want to do and accomplish.

Do you realize that you talk to yourself? Psychologists say we all talk to ourselves. They call it "self-talk," apparently—that's the technical term. Seriously though, the experts say we are talking to ourselves all the time. We have 50,000 to 70,000 thoughts per day.

Let that register for just a minute: 50,000 to 70,000 thoughts each and every day. And the experts say the overwhelming number of those, 98 or 99 percent of our thoughts, are habitual, meaning they are largely the same thoughts we had yesterday and the day before and the day before that. We think essentially about the same things, and in the same way, every day.

But finally, here is the statistic that really caught my attention: the Cleveland Clinic estimates that 80 percent of our thoughts are negative. Again, allow me to repeat this for emphasis: 80 percent of our thoughts are negative!

So, the question is not: Do you talk to yourself? The question is: What do you say when you talk to yourself? How do you allow your thoughts to direct your life? Is it 80 percent negative?

Norman Vincent Peale tells the story of being in Hong Kong and walking by a tattoo parlor. He found it interesting to look at all the variety of tattoos. One in particular caught his eye. It said, "Born to Lose."

Peale was aghast and went inside to ask the Chinese artist, "Does anyone really have that tattooed on his body?" And the artist said, "Sometimes."

"I just can't believe anyone would do that," Peale said.

And the artist, in his broken English, said, "Before tattoo on body, tattoo on mind."

The words we speak to ourselves have this tremendous power over us. We may scoff at the notion of ever getting a tattoo reading, "Born to Lose." Yet the words we say to ourselves habitually, day after day, when any obstacle or opportunity presents itself, might be, "I can't," "I'll fail," "I'll lose."

Eventually, we might carry around deep in our hearts the words, "I'm a failure," "I'm a loser," "I was born to lose."

I remember talking to a man years ago about the minor surgery his wife was soon going to have, and he said, "She's already planning how this isn't going to work out for her." I knew her and knew she had said those words, or words like them, to herself continuously over the years; she had reinforced them deep inside her for her whole life, and it was obvious in everything she did and in how her life was turning out.

There was a man who would almost always buy his gasoline at the same station at the same time during the week. This was before pumps were computerized to accept credit cards, so he would interact with the cashier, and it was usually the same young man. The first time he met this cashier, he absentmindedly asked, "How's it going?"

Without looking up, the attendant responded, "Lousy." It was clear he didn't want to talk about it, so the customer just smiled and gave him his money. The next week, the man asked the same question, and the cashier again said, "Lousy." This went on for months. It became a despairing little liturgy they would repeat every week.

Then one day the young attendant startled the customer. He had asked him once again, "How's it going?" and braced for the usual response. But this time the cashier smiled and exclaimed, "Great!"

Astonished, the man asked, "So, things are improving?"

"Nah," he responded, "I'm just lowering my expectations."

What do you say when you talk to yourself? I like to think of it this way: the words we speak to ourselves have the power to help us be either a thermometer or a thermostat. A thermometer, of course, reflects the temperature in the room; it tells you whether it's hot or cold, gives you a reading on what it's like outside or in the building or room where you are.

My observation is that most people are like thermometers. They reflect what is going on around them, what the circumstances of their lives are. If the environment around them is not so good, then they are sure not to be so good either. And if things are going well, they may reflect a more positive outlook themselves. But just as likely, they often still give a reading of the mostly negative thoughts and words that inhabit their mind.

I was outside on a beautiful spring day recently and I overheard someone say, "We're going to pay for this nice weather. There's probably a storm coming!" I wish I could say this is the only time an amazing day had been interrupted by such a comment. I'm embarrassed to say I've been known to throw an unwarranted and unnecessarily discouraging word out there, too.

On the other hand, a thermostat sets the temperature; it creates the environment, it's in charge of the hot and cold and changes to what is needed and best for the room and setting. Far fewer people are like thermostats. To be a thermostat, you don't simply reflect the environment around you; you help to create the environment.

People who are thermostats don't sit and wait for life to happen to them. They cause life to happen. If a situation is not so good, they don't just reflect that; they give energy and hope to the situation, they reveal what might be possible.

Scott Peck, the eminent psychiatrist who wrote the best-selling book *The Road Less Traveled*, uses the concepts of immaturity and maturity similarly to my use of thermometer and thermostat. He writes, "… it seems to me what characterizes most immature people is that they sit around complaining that life doesn't meet their demands. … But what characterizes those relative few who are fully mature is that they regard it as their responsibility—even as an opportunity—to meet life's demands."

So how do you stop being a thermometer—merely reflecting what is going on in your life, the sometimes positive but mostly negative thoughts and words that habitually inhabit your mind—and become a thermostat?

Well, it's not easy. You have to work at it. It may take a long time, maybe a lifetime. You have to want to change your life and the habitual thoughts and words that control you. You have to speak words that go against the grain of the 80 percent negative self-talk and create something new and different in your life. Turn the habitually negative into something that is habitually positive and productive and hopeful.

Try this: intentionally expose yourself to words that are positive and hopeful. It's not just that these are words that are full of optimism and wishful thinking, it's that they are more productive and meaningful for creating and growing into the kind of person you want to be. They are words that set you in a certain, more fruitful, direction; they help to establish a destination, a destiny, for your life.

Do you remember the novel, later turned into a movie, *The Cider House Rules*, by John Irving? Much of the story is set in an orphanage in Maine during the Great Depression and World War II. Times are tough, and the notion is inescapable—it's meant to be there in the story—that these children stuck in this orphanage have hardly any chance at all in life. Only the young, perfectly healthy ones ever seem to get chosen by the happy couples who visit; most of the children are growing older (and in at least one case sicker) and less likely by the day to ever be adopted. At some point, they will be turned out into a world where they have no future.

This is the environment of the story. But every night, the doctor in the orphanage, played by Michael Caine in the movie, stands outside the door of the room where the boys have gone to bed and calls in to them, "Good night you princes of Maine, you kings of New England!"

Now these boys aren't the princes of anything, they aren't kings, and I'm sure they don't even know what the good doctor is trying to do. But he has set the thermostat; this powerful, habitual affirmation is reverberating around in their minds and in their souls. We don't know what ever happens to any of the boys, of course—this work of fiction ends with them still in the orphanage—but it's not hard to believe that they will one day amount to something good and maybe even great.

Frank Szymanski played football as an offensive lineman for Notre Dame years ago. One day he was called to testify in a civil lawsuit. On the stand, he was asked by the judge, "How good are you?" Frank replied, "Please don't ask me that." But the judge persisted, asking again and demanding an answer. So Frank said, "I am the best offensive lineman who has ever played at Notre Dame."

The next day he was back on campus when he ran into head coach Frank Leahy. Coach Leahy asked Frank if he really told the judge he was the best offensive lineman who has ever played for Notre Dame? Frank replied that he did. His coach then asked why he said that, and Frank responded, "Well, I didn't want to, but I was under oath."

I love that, and my guess is that Frank was telling himself how great of a lineman he was long before he lived into it and became the greatest. He may not have wanted to say so publicly for fear of sounding embarrassingly arrogant in front of his coach and teammates, but he no doubt reinforced those notions of doing his best and being the best until they came true.

What words would set an overall new course for your life? What words would help to redefine a new direction? What if you were to choose a small selection of words and phrases and repeat them periodically throughout the day, things like: "I'm a person of worth." "I'm a child of God." "The world has need of me." "My life is filled with possibility." "I choose hope." "I can make a difference." "My smile can make someone feel better." "Today is a new adventure."

Doing this every day, repeating these phrases to yourself and perhaps meditating on what they mean, can begin to reset the thermostat in your life, can start to crowd out and decrease the percentage of your negative and destructive thoughts. I suggest you say these or similar words to yourself every day, maybe write them on Post-it notes and place them strategically around your office or home, and then watch how your life begins to change. Carry them around with you in a pocket, so you remember every time you pull them out to read or just put your hand in your pocket and touch them with your fingers. The goal is to internalize these words and the thoughts and feelings they produce, the direction they foster, and watch your life begin to change.

In addition, quotes from famous people can jumpstart some positive energy. For example:

> "In the middle of difficulty lies opportunity," by Albert Einstein.
>
> "Believe you can and you're halfway there," by Theodore Roosevelt.
>
> "Whether you think you can or think you can't, you're right!" by Henry Ford.
>
> "You must do the thing you think you cannot do," by Eleanor Roosevelt.
>
> "I can't go on. I'll go on," by Samuel Beckett, the playwright.

It's easy to find many more of these types of inspiring quotes on the Internet by simply Googling things like "encouraging quotes" or "hopeful quotes," and seeing what comes up.

Perhaps the best quote I've ever heard was someone who told me, "You have everything you need right here," as he tapped me in the chest. "You just have to believe in yourself."

I've thought about that one a lot over the years, especially when I have felt disappointed or discouraged, like I wasn't getting anywhere. I have everything I need right here, inside me—everything I need to be happy, everything I need to be successful, everything I need to figure out what to do next, everything I need to find meaning and purpose. Every time I think of that quote from someone who was never famous and whose face I can hardly remember—I didn't know him very well—I do begin once again to believe and move forward.

Sometimes it's the people you've never heard of who say the most worthwhile things. So always be listening to what others have to say; wisdom can come from the most unlikely source.

Verses from the Bible can also provide words to speak to yourself to guide you in a positive way. I have always been a big fan of memorizing helpful verses and then calling them to mind. Here are some examples of the verses I turn to:

> "I can do all things through him (God) who gives me the strength." (Philippians 4:13)

> "For I know the plans I have for you, says the Lord, plans for your welfare and not for harm, to give you hope and a future." (Jeremiah 29:11)

> "The Lord is my light and my salvation; whom shall I fear? The Lord is the stronghold of my life; of whom shall I be afraid?" (Psalm 27:1)

> "This one thing I do: forgetting what lies behind and straining forward to what lies ahead, I press on toward the goal…" (Philippians 3:13-14)

I don't know about you, but when I say those words to myself, I sit up straighter, I feel I have more power and more of a purpose, I want to get up and do something monumental and good. The Bible is an amazing resource for finding words that give you courage and upliftment and hope.

I so fondly remember one minister who always seemed to have the right pastoral word for any situation. He once told a woman who had come out of surgery, "Now, I know the doctor has given you some prescriptions for pain and other things, but I want to give you a prescription, too. Read Psalm 103 every morning when you wake up and every night when you go to bed." Then he recited a few key verses from memory: "Bless the Lord, O my soul, and do not forget all his benefits—who forgives all your iniquity, who heals all your diseases, who redeems your life from the Pit, who crowns you with steadfast love and mercy, who satisfies you with good as long as you live so that your youth is renewed like the eagle's." Just his saying those words had a visible calming—dare

I say healing—effect on the woman. You could tell this was going to be a prescription she would return to every morning and night.

I have also known those who were ill who held onto these words from Isaiah 43 for dear life: "Descendants of Jacob, I, the Lord, created you and formed you. Israel, don't be afraid. I have rescued you. I have called you by name; now you belong to me. When you cross deep rivers, I will be with you, and you won't drown. When you walk through fire, you won't be burned or scorched in the flames."

Especially those enduring the damaging, sometimes burning, side effects of radiation treatment or chemotherapy for cancer grasp firmly to those words, "When you walk through fire…" There are many sources for healing and encouraging words out there, especially in the Bible.

Poetry can be another place to turn for words that are energizing and revitalizing. One poem I love is "Don't Quit" by Edgar Guest:

> When things go wrong, as they sometimes will,
> When the road you're trudging seems all uphill,
> When the funds are low and the debts are high,
> And you want to smile, but you have to sigh,
> When care is pressing you down a bit
> Rest if you must, but don't you quit.
> Life is queer with its twists and turns,
> As everyone of us sometimes learns,
> And many a failure turns about
> When they might have won, if they'd stuck it out.
> Don't give up though the pace seems slow,
> You may succeed with another blow.
> Often the struggler has given up
> When he might have captured the victor's cup;
> And he learned too late when the night came down,
> How close he was to the golden crown.
> Success is failure turned inside out
> The silver tint of the clouds of doubt
> And you never can tell how close you are,
> It may be near when it seems so far;
> So stick to the fight when you're hardest hit,
> It's when things seem worst that you mustn't quit.

Not only is the message that you may be closer to success than you realize a truth you need to hear, just repeating the words, "don't quit," "don't you quit," "you mustn't quit," has a penetrating and invigorating effect on one's demeanor and attitude. I don't know about you, but I am instantly transformed.

The same is true when I recite Emily Dickinson's famous little poem:

> Hope is the thing with feathers
> That perches in the soul,
> That sings the tune without the words,
> And never stops at all.

I have to honestly say that I don't know what in the world she is talking about here. And yet, somehow, I do. Not intellectually perhaps, but something is perched in my soul and given flight when I say the poem aloud or silently to myself. Hope is there, lurking and ready to be released, and I am calling it forth with these words.

Here then, are my suggestions for inhabiting your brain with words that will inspire you to new heights. Create a statement or phrase that is motivating and empowering. Find a quote from someone famous or not-so-famous that speaks to you. Locate a verse from the Bible that brings healing and encouragement. Discover lines of poetry that are stirring and challenging. Combine these and other maxims from various sources, edit them, concoct your own, personalize them, as the best and most hopeful and exceptional expressions that are right for you at this moment in time.

The point is to have solid and galvanizing words of strength and hope that come quickly to your mind to say to yourself, to internalize, to counter those words that are negative and defeating, and to motivate you to move forward.

I think it is wise every once in a while to stop and simply ask yourself, "What am I saying to myself?" "Are the words I am speaking to myself thermometer words or thermostat words?"

Be completely honest. It's not helpful if you try to make yourself look better to yourself than you really are. By being aware of the internal monologue that is going on, especially when it is negative, you can begin to challenge those words and thoughts.

It's one thing to know in theory that 80 percent of self-talk is negative for the average person, but it's something else to come to the realization that you are speaking so destructively to yourself. Ask yourself if that is really the way you want to speak to yourself. Perhaps sometimes it will be, but most of the time it is not.

So, re-think what you are doing. Object to what you are saying to yourself. Ask, "What are the consequences of speaking to myself so negatively? Where is this leading me?" Staying this course with your automatic, go-to, negative self-talk may be leading to personal or professional failure and maybe even disaster. The objective is to consciously replace such words with ones that are positive and healthy and constructive.

For example, your first reaction may be "I can't do this," to anything you're asked to do and even to some things that you yourself have a real desire to do. This may simply be your instinctual, gut reaction every time you face anything challenging. The task may be straightforward, but still your response to yourself is, "I can't do this." This knee-jerk reaction creates a mental block that keeps you from accomplishing it.

I don't want to make it sound simple because you have to overcome years of negative conditioning, but you need to change that conditioning by forcefully and continuously telling yourself, "I can do this." You have to replace "I can't do this," with "I can do this." Often this is enough to create the energy and attitude to accomplish the job.

Sometimes though, the thing you are being asked to do, or asking of yourself, is downright difficult. Just psyching yourself into a can-do attitude is not enough. You then not only have to tell yourself, "I can do this," but also tell yourself how you can do this: "I can do this because I will learn how to do this." Or, "I will practice until I am able to do this." "I will get help to do this." "I will work hard to be able to do this." "I will work harder than I have ever worked in my life to do this."

It may be that you really cannot accomplish it right now. So, you say to yourself, "I will one day be able to do this." You might even need to break down the steps you will take to be able to accomplish it: "I will do X, Y, and Z first and then I will be able to do this." Pretty soon, you will be doing it.

There will probably always be that natural tendency to think negatively in the first moments when a challenge occurs. Those obstructive words and thoughts will always be there, lurking in the background, waiting to take over if given a chance. One clinical psychologist calls them, "Unruly passengers in the backseat of the car you're driving."

You have to catch yourself before they take control and lead you wildly in the wrong direction, and instead realize what you are doing and intentionally begin to speak words that set your mind in a different, positive direction, and perhaps even describe to yourself the specific strategic steps you can take to accomplish the task at hand. In this way, again according to this clinical psychologist, "You

hear the noise and ruckus behind you [from the unruly passengers in the back-seat], but you keep your attention focused on the road ahead."

Years ago, after a dinner at a Chinese restaurant, I opened a fortune cookie that said, "Act as though it were impossible to fail." It may sound ludicrous to put much stock in a fortune cookie, but I took these words to heart. Whenever I faced a difficult situation or difficult people, I would pull out those words and say them to myself.

I actually kept the little piece of paper with the fortune on it for a while and literally pulled it out of my pocket when I needed it. I eventually lost it, but by then I could readily call it to mind when needed.

I don't really think of them at any other time, but when there is a meeting or a person who makes me apprehensive, I automatically think of those words and square my shoulders and practically march in to where I need to be, having set myself up for a situation where I feel like I cannot fail.

The journalist and writer Regina Brett describes a man she knows who is about as upbeat as they come. I'm not sure he was always this way, but he now lives by two simple words: *Get to*. Instead of saying, "I have to," he says, "I get to." You and I can try this too.

See how it works for daily tasks that can sometimes get to the point where they feel routine and burdensome. So, for instance, instead of telling yourself, "I have to go to work today," you could say, "I get to go to work today." I get to have a career and vocation. I get to fill my day with work that has meaning and purpose. I get to be a contributing member of society and provide financially for myself and my family.

Or, instead of saying to yourself, "I have to go to the grocery store," you could say, "I get to go to the grocery store." I get to go to a place that sells every kind of food you can imagine; not everyone has this opportunity. I get to choose what food I will eat, to pick out what is good and nutritious but also something sweet that will drive my palate wild.

Instead of telling yourself, "I have to take the kids to soccer practice," you could say, "I get to take the kids to soccer practice." I get to spend time with these precious children that I brought into the world and that I love. I get to pour my life into them and make an imprint on them. If I don't get distracted with less important things, I get to be with them all the time, and I hope never to take them for granted.

Have to are thermometer words. *Get to* are thermostat words. I can think of no better way for you to capture a different perspective on your life, gain more control, and find meaning in what you do and who you are than to boldly switch from saying *have to* to *get to*. It works for everything, Regina Brett claims.

Try it on what you regard as your biggest challenge. It has made all the difference in the world for this man she describes, and I think it will for you and me too.

Step One

Ask yourself at any given moment, "What am I saying to myself? Is it mostly negative? Are my words more thermometer words or thermostat?" Make the decision to be a thermostat. Believe you can do it. Create positive, hopeful, and resilient words and phrases for your life in general and for specific instances where you know you will need them when things happen and you're tempted to turn automatically negative and defeatist. Say *get to* instead of *have to* for some of the more burdensome tasks in your life.

Michael Phelps at the 2016 Summer Olympics in Rio de Janeiro.

TO LOOK OR TO SEE

Believe In Your Vision

One of the most striking psychological studies I've ever read about comes out of the Cleveland Clinic and compares ordinary, everyday people who are engaged in an exercise program at the gym.

Some of them actually went to the gym to perform certain arm and finger exercises, but others only visualized those exercises in their minds. It will come as no surprise that those who went through the exercise program increased their strength—on average, they grew about 30 percent stronger in those muscles. What fascinates me, though, is that those who simply visualized lifting the weights and working out also grew stronger. They grew stronger on average by almost 15 percent in an elbow flexion exercise and 35 percent in a finger abduction exercise.

I have to say that I was astounded by this. They never lifted a weight, never set foot in a gym, never put forth an ounce of physical effort, and yet they grew stronger by a measurable amount. They grew stronger because they could see themselves grow stronger.

A lot of research has been done in recent years on visualization in athletics, and it has been found that mental practice is almost as effective as actual physical practice. Brain studies now show that thoughts produce the same instructions to the mind as actions. One study on professional weightlifters showed that the brain patterns activated when they lifted hundreds of pounds during their workouts were similarly activated when they only imagined lifting. The brain is getting trained for the actual performance during visualization. Many seasoned athletes in every sport use vivid, highly detailed internal images and run-throughs of their performance, engaging all their senses in the mental rehearsal.

At one point, I was working with the New Orleans Saints professional football team in the early 2000s. One of the young players, Darren Howard, came to me for some advice on how to mentally prepare for the next game.

I told him to visualize some of the plays he would make during the game: making tackles, blocking passes (he was a defensive player). Specifically, I told him to picture himself rushing the quarterback, stripping the ball from him, picking it up, and running for a touchdown. He promised to mentally rehearse this image throughout the week.

I watched the game on TV that weekend, being particularly interested to watch Darren play. He was playing at his usual high level of performance but seemed extra-motivated. Midway through the third quarter, I watched as he rushed the quarterback, stripped the ball from him, picked it up, and ran for a touchdown.

I think my mouth was slightly open as he crossed the goal line; I couldn't quite believe it. On the other hand, after encouraging him to picture it just exactly this way all week, it seemed inevitable. When I came to visit the team in practice that week, Darren was waiting for me by the entrance. "Help me picture something else for this week!" he said excitedly.

"Whatever you visualize, you materialize," is how some people have phrased it. The phrase I use is a similar concept but talks more specifically to what is happening scientifically: "Neurons that fire together wire together." What this means is that we are beginning to realize in the field of psychology that there is a neuroplasticity to our brains. They form and mold easily; they shape and re-shape themselves daily.

Your brain is a bunch of neurons, little pieces of matter that send messages to each other. And the messages you send begin to wire your brain in a certain way. What we think about and see in our mind's eye begins to wire the brain to see it, too. If we understand this and take command of it, if we are intentional and deliberate in the way we think and what we think about, if we visualize an outcome over and over, it begins to re-wire our brain to see it and believe it will happen.

This can have a profound effect on our minds and consequently on our lives. We can become so much more than we are right now. We can become what we see.

Jack Nicklaus was once quoted as saying, "I never hit a shot, not even in practice, without having a very sharp, in-focus picture of it in my head. First, I see the ball where I want it to finish, nice and white and sitting up high on the bright green grass. Then the scene quickly changes, and I see the ball getting there; its path, trajectory, and shape, even its behavior on landing. Then there is a sort of fadeout, and the next scene shows me taking the kind of swing that will make the previous images into reality." Nicklaus has won more Majors than anyone in history. And he saw each win, each step, each swing, each shot over and over in his mind, until it became a reality.

One of the greatest athletes of our time, and of all time, is swimmer Michael Phelps. He has competed in five Olympics and is the most decorated Olympian ever, winning 23 gold medals and 28 medals overall. He had a great coach, Bob Bowman, during his formative years of training. At the end of each practice, Bowman would tell Michael, then just a teenager, to go home and, "Watch the videotape. Watch it before you go to sleep and watch it when you wake up."

It wasn't a real videotape; it was a mental visualization of the perfect race. Each night and each morning, Michael would imagine himself swimming the perfect race: every detail, every stroke,

Golfing great Jack Nicklaus said he never takes a shot "without having a very sharp, in-focus picture of it in my head."

every second of the race. During practice, Bowman would shout, "Put in the videotape!" and Michael would push himself to swim that perfect race that was in his mind. He got faster and faster.

Eventually, on game day, all Bowman had to do before a race was whisper, "Get the videotape ready," and Michael Phelps would go out and crush the competition.

During the Olympics in Beijing in 2008, Michael dove off the starting blocks and into the water for his fourth race, the 200-meter butterfly—he'd already won three gold medals. He knew something was wrong as soon as he hit the water. There was moisture in his goggles; they were leaking.

By the second turn, everything was blurry. By the third turn and final lap, his goggles were completely filled with water; he couldn't see anything. Most swimmers would have panicked, but Michael was calm. Some of the videotapes in his mind had featured problems like this. He had mentally rehearsed how to respond if his goggles failed.

As he started his last lap, he estimated how many strokes he needed—19 or 20, maybe 21—and started counting. He was relaxed and swam at full strength. At 18 strokes, he started anticipating the wall.

He could hear the crowd cheering but couldn't see anything, so he had no idea who they were cheering for. He made one last huge stroke, then he reached for, and touched, the wall.

Michael Phelps began visualizing the "perfect" race as a young swimmer, helping him grow to be the most decorated Olympian in history.

When he ripped his goggles off and looked up at the scoreboard, it said "World Record" by his name. He'd won another gold medal.

After the race, a reporter asked him what it felt like to swim blind, and he said, "It felt like I imagined it would."

To see the outcome, to picture every action you will perform in order to arrive there, to rehearse it again and again, to imagine the obstacles and opposition and how you will overcome them, to allow your mind to visualize what might be and how you will get there—it's not just for athletes and sporting endeavors. Visualization can help you become the kind of person you want to be and accomplish the kinds of things you want to accomplish. It can lead you in a certain direction with your life and to a certain destination. To not just look at who you are now, or who others think you are, or what your circumstances are, but to fully see in your mind's eye what you might one day be, is really quite an amazing thing. "Neurons that fire together wire together" is a truth that can apply to anyone and any undertaking.

I think of those, for example, who are creating something brand new. The world has never experienced anything like it before. It's being invented, made up, generated, where there had been nothing. Someone had to see it first before it could ever be revealed to the rest of us.

Beethoven used to wander in the woods to give life to his music. There were no instruments or musicians, just the beauty of nature and what was going on in his mind. In the studio of his brain he saw and heard great symphonies of sound, the notes dancing around, marching up and down on the screen of his imagination.

When James Watt's crude steam engine worked for the first time, he shouted excitedly to his friends, "You see it working now with your physical eye, but long ago I saw it working in my mind's eye."

Walt Disney had the vision for Disney World but died several years before it welcomed its first visitors. At the grand opening ceremony, one speaker said, "I just wish Walt had been here to see this," to which his widow Lillian, when it was her turn to speak, replied, "Walt did see this; that's why it's here."

Steve Jobs, the founder of Apple, believed very strongly in what he called his "reality distortion field." He didn't see what the reality was right then, he saw what the reality could be. When the iPhone was first developed, his vision was for a whole new kind of glass, which he called gorilla glass—and he needed this new glass in six months. The engineers said it couldn't be done, it was impossible, they didn't have the capacity, this kind of glass didn't exist, it hadn't been invented yet. But Jobs, in his own persuasive and demanding way, said to the engineers, "Yes, you can do it. Don't be afraid. Get your mind around it. You can do it." And they did then begin to get their minds around it, they did see it, and produced this glass that hadn't yet been invented in less than six months.

There is an old poem I like, by an anonymous author, that heralds the potential of enormous audacity in our imagination:

> For man is a dreamer ever,
> He glimpses the hills afar,
> And plans for the things out yonder
> Where all his tomorrows are;
> And back of the sound of the hammer,
> And back of the hissing steam,
> And back of the hand on the throttle
> Is ever a daring dream.

In a very real way, this is what you can do with your life—whatever your pursuit might be. Do you ever pause and ask: What am I trying to create with my life? Is it something I not only want to do, but feel I *have to* do? Not only would I like to accomplish it, but feel I must. Is there some goal I have? Some purpose that is calling me? Is there a daring dream behind it all? Can I see it happening? Can I picture myself there? Can I envision the concrete steps it will take to get there? Can I imagine the people who will be helped and encouraged and inspired and maybe even saved by what I will do?

One of my favorite recent series of commercials is of young people, high school or college age, having a discussion with their parents about going into the military. But the conversation is not held in the abstract. For the young people at least, they are present in the very place where they will be serving. They can picture where they will be and what they will do and who they'll be with.

To the parent, it's just a career in the military, which may not sound all that promising, but the young people are seeing themselves as a technician in a huge control room helping to use the latest satellite-tracking technology, or as a medic on a relief mission in a disaster zone of a foreign country, saving a child's life. They see their exhilarating and indispensable roles and vividly begin to create the pictures of them for their parents, too.

Can you see where you will be and what you will do to get there? Can you picture the obstacles and perhaps even the opponents that will inevitably be part of your journey, and how you will go around or through them? This is a big one on any journey of faith into the future: the obstacles and opposition.

Like Michael Phelps and the goggles, being able to work through the difficulties and struggles to reach your daring dream, being willing to take a risk at some point, despite the odds against you, will largely determine whether you succeed or fail.

Victor Frankl had been a psychiatrist in Vienna before World War II. But during the war, as a Jew, he was thrown into the Auschwitz concentration camp by the Nazi regime. The conditions there were simply incomprehensible; I'm convinced that it's impossible for us who weren't there to ever grasp the depth of the horror, surrounded every moment by death and violence and cruelty and starvation.

Almost no one who entered through the gates of this place, which was as close to hell on earth as we can imagine, ever emerged from it. Almost everyone perished. But Frankl survived. After the war, he lived for 50 more years, into his 90s. And he survived, in part, because he would picture himself one day lecturing to others about his experience in Auschwitz, and how he survived, and how they too could survive their struggles. He saw himself speaking to others, in lecture halls and auditoriums, every day, over and over. This image of what his life could be was a reality so vivid in his mind that after the war it actually became his life.

Nelson Mandela was put in prison by the government of South Africa for his revolutionary activities against the racist Apartheid system. For 27 years he was imprisoned, and for much of that time he was held at the notorious Robben Island, where he spent his days in hard labor, mindlessly and endlessly breaking rocks into gravel or working in a lime quarry. Yet he maintained his unique vision for what a free South Africa could ultimately look like, which allowed him to live that vision of this freedom once he was released and became the first president of his post-Apartheid country. I heard one person claim that because Mandela's mind was so set on what the future could be, "While he was in prison, he was the only truly free person in the whole country."

Natan Sharansky, a mathematician and computer scientist in the Soviet Union, spent nine years in prison, accused of being a spy for the United States. While in solitary confinement, he played himself in mental chess. He had no board or pieces; he pictured each move and counter-move in his mind. He said, "I might as well use the opportunity to become the world champion."

Remarkably, several years later he got the chance to play and beat world champion chess player (many think the greatest player of all time) Garry Kasparov.

Visualizing can be a powerful way to overcome, or learn from and grow in the midst of, our obstacles and opposition. I hope you will never be placed in a prison like what I have described above for these three incredible individuals, but there will be a prison of some sort that you will have to face, a feeling of being imprisoned in some set of circumstances that will threaten to discourage and defeat you. We have to see ourselves in ultimate triumph over our prisons, experiencing growth and moving forward.

Nothing is as destructive to us as fear. Fear of failure, fear of loss, fear of rejection, fear of change, fear of death; the list of things we fear is pretty endless. If something could possibly go wrong, no matter how remote it may be, we can be, and often are, afraid of it.

In fact, it's the fear of the thing that might happen more than the thing itself actually happening that can be so crippling. We conjure up such vivid images of the bad things that are out there waiting for us.

One of my favorite cartoons—I don't remember just precisely where I got it—shows a burglar holding up a man in his home. The man has his hands up as the burglar is walking out with a bag of loot. At the last minute, the man says, "Can you come upstairs? I'd like you to meet my wife. She's been expecting you every night for the last 30 years."

The message of the cartoon is clear: fear can capture our imagination and hold onto us for years, and it may be worse than the actual thing we fear, even if it does eventually occur. It was Mark Twain who said, "I have experienced some terrible things in my life, some of which actually happened."

That phrase, "Neurons that fire together wire together," is at work here too, but if we're not careful, it can drive us in a completely negative and devastating direction. Remember the 80 percent negative self-talk that can become habitual, as mentioned in the first chapter? That principle is in operation here as well. The neuroplasticity of our brains means that they can be wired for fear and doubt and worry.

In fact, the original wiring of our brains seems to be toward negative thoughts, and overwhelmingly so. In prehistoric and primitive cultures this was very much a good thing. A tiger could actually attack you at any moment back in those days, so you had better have a built-in fear mechanism that kept you ever on the alert. If something bad happened, you had to remember it so you didn't repeat it.

The brain, in this sense, is an outdated organ, like your tonsils or appendix; it doesn't want you to be successful or happy, it simply wants you to survive.

Where this leaves us today, though, is with a brain fully equipped with a standard package of fear, doubt, worry, failure, and everything negative. When we take a look at what is more or less automatically in our brains, what we usually are looking at are images of bad things happening to us pretty much in every direction. It's like our brains are Velcro for the bad; we have a certain built-in inferiority complex. It's almost normal for you to be negative and full of fear. I once heard a comedian say, "I was telling myself that my brain is the most amazing organ in my body, then I realized who was telling me that."

One of the most haunting illustrations I've ever come across is the story of a man who was thrown into a prisoner of war camp during World War II. (I realize that this is the fourth story I've used in this chapter that has to do with a prison, but I think all four, perhaps especially this one, hold a certain, poignant insight.) Of course, many in the camp didn't make it, but he survived and did so, in large part, because he was imagining what he would do after the war.

Before the war, he'd been in a business of some kind and he'd done well, made a good living. But for him, it wasn't a good *life*; he hated it, every day he hated going to work, and this had taken its toll.

But in the camp, he re-thought his life and thought if he survived he could start over. He remembered that in his younger years he had always wanted to be an artist. He was good at it but in order to make money, he went into business, which led to the job he had now, which was killing his soul. In that POW camp, there and then, he decided that he would become an artist. He would survive, he would emerge one day, and he would live his dream. It was what he was meant to do.

So every day, for hours on end, in the midst of otherwise unbearable hardship, he saw himself as an artist, he visualized himself at his easel, he pictured himself drawing and painting, and imagined the kinds of things he would create. And he survived.

After the war, he was reunited with his wife. Of course, he quickly began to share the excitement over his vision with her. He told her what he saw of himself as an artist and of the kinds of things he would paint. At some point, she interrupted him with a kind of laugh, "You'll never make any money at that. You're no artist. I'm glad these crazy ideas kept you alive, but you've got to go back into business now and back to the way things were. You've got to give up all of these foolish thoughts."

The man turned his face away from his wife, looked out the window, and never said another word to her about it—and was dead in two weeks.

In a way, we can't really blame this man's wife (it may be exactly what would come naturally for you and me too in the same situation). She was simply acting out her own negative visualization and self-talk as it had been wired into her brain. But, as I say, this story haunts me. It's a warning that this negative visualization that is often our go-to perspective can stunt our growth as human beings and have a crippling effect on our lives. We have to be conscious of what we're doing because picturing what we want our lives to be can be arbitrary and careless and thoughtless, even ultimately destructive, and we can force those images onto others.

It haunts me perhaps most to know that there is such a power at my command, and I don't always use it; most often I just waste it. It's there all the time: the power to create, to heal, to love, to forgive, to be bold, to be happy, to change direction, to overcome any fear, to determine my own future in spite of the circumstances.

James Allen, one of the early pioneers in this way of thinking, wrote in his classic little book, *As a Man Thinketh*, "A man cannot directly choose his circumstances, but he can choose his thoughts, and so indirectly, yet surely, shape his circumstances." We have to remember from the story of the man in the POW camp that he created a vivid image of himself that gave him hope and life. He might easily have given up and died in the POW camp, but instead his years there were quite possibly the best of his life. Whatever his failure to even attempt to shape the circumstances of his life after the war, he was certainly able to use the power of his vision and thoughts to shape the awful circumstances of his prison.

You and I can do the same thing. There is this unstoppable power that we have ever with us. It is the power to simply think about things, to send messages to our minds, to visualize, to picture, to wire our brains in a way that is more hopeful and productive. It is the power to see—not just to look at what is there right now, but to see what might be.

I have this power and so do you. But we have to recognize it and seize it. We have to believe in it and put it to work.

We always have a choice as to which thoughts we will allow to occupy our mind, which vision we will obey and trust and live. The legend is told of a traveler who stopped at the edge of a city and asked a farmer who was working in the field, "What kind of people live in this city up ahead? I have it in my mind to settle here." The farmer asked, "Well, what kind of people did you live with before?" And the traveler said, "Oh, in the city I come from the people were narrow-minded and self-centered and difficult. I couldn't wait to get out of there." To this the farmer replied, "Then I'm sorry, but you'll find the same kind of people here." So, the traveler decided not to settle there; he bypassed the city and moved on.

A second traveler came along presently and stopped and asked the farmer, "What kind of people live in this city up ahead? I have it in my mind to settle here." And the farmer asked again, "Well, what kind of people did you live with before?" With a wistful smile, this traveler said, "Oh, those people were the finest in the world. Only business reasons have forced me to leave. I would have stayed there happily." The farmer replied, "Then I'm happy to tell you that you'll find the same kind of people here."

So much of our life depends on our outlook and attitude. So much depends on the perception and internal foresight we have of ourselves and others. Once we understand this, we can choose the kind of thoughts we will fill our minds with and the kind of vision we will believe in and pursue.

There's an old story about two shoe salesmen who were sent to a remote country to open up a new market there. Three days after their arrival, the first salesman sent a cablegram (this was back in the day) that read: "Returning home on next plane. Can't possibly sell shoes here. Everybody goes barefoot!"

Nothing was heard from the second salesman for about two weeks, and everyone wondered what he could be doing in a land that held such poor prospects. Finally, a fat airmail envelope with this message for the home office arrived: "Fifty orders enclosed! Many more to come! Prospects unlimited! Great opportunity! Nobody here has shoes!" You can tell simply by the exclamation points which salesman was full of a vision he believed in.

There is always an option. The door to thinking differently is always there to be opened. There is always a way—in any circumstance, facing any situation—to turn away from simply being the thermometer and to become the thermostat. The key is to see it in your mind so it can become your reality.

We have been talking a great deal about identifying in the habits of your mind a specific objective you desire to achieve. Things like running a fumble for a touchdown, or creating gorilla glass, or surviving a concentration camp. Or more likely for you and me, it will be less dramatic, but just as thrilling objectives like getting that diploma or reaching for that career or working hard for that promotion. It is important to see it and go for it!

It is just as critical, maybe even more so for your ultimate happiness and well-being, to set your inner thoughts toward an overall, beneficial framework for your life and intentionally turn your attention in an uplifting and encouraging direction.

Paul, in the book of Philippians from the Bible, gives us some good advice when he tells us how to develop a more positive and hopeful mind. He writes, "Finally, beloved, whatever is true, whatever is honorable, whatever is just, whatever is pure, whatever is pleasing, whatever is commendable, if there is any excellence and if there is anything worthy of praise, think about these things." A different translation that I like of the same verses is, "I'd say you'll do best by filling your minds and meditating on things true, noble, reputable, authentic, compelling, gracious—the best, not the worst; the beautiful, not the ugly; things to praise, not things to curse."

One simple practice that can have a profound effect on your daily life is to think of those things for which you are grateful. It's been said that happy people are grateful people. So, think of things for which you give thanks. Maybe it's something general that you often overlook: the air you breathe, the sun on your face, the change of season. Or maybe it's a good memory; life has its ups and downs, but that moment from the past was really an uplifting moment. And then think of what has happened in your day; think of what you specifically have to be grateful for. Each member of your family, a list of friends and what each one means to you, the work that you have right now, the challenge of it even though it can sometimes be overwhelming, the familiar voice you spoke with, the walk you took with someone you love, watching children play. The list can really be quite endless, and it can begin to re-wire your brain and help you think in a different way and send your life in a new direction.

A man by the name of Roger was diagnosed with metastatic lymphoma and told he was in the end stage of life. He was confined to his bedroom and received daily home nursing care, including a morphine drip to manage the pain. A friend came by one day, and Roger was saying how he felt so helpless and worthless. So, his friend asked, "How can you still find a way to live and serve even in the midst of this adversity?"

Roger had no answer; his thoughts were all discouraged and depressed at this stage. But his friend asked, "Have you shared with other people the lessons you've learned in your rich and full life?" Roger was silent at first, but gradually his face brightened and his skin color went from ashen to vibrant and healthy pink. He sat up straighter in bed. He smiled. "I could write letters," he said. "That's something I could do."

So, he did. He wrote letters of gratitude to old friends and colleagues, to teachers, to his family. He wrote letters to his grandchildren, thanking them for carrying on the family traditions. And then he began to pass along some of the wisdom he had gained in life, talking to them about various things like persistence and how to handle failure. He wrote to them about God. He didn't tell them to believe in God, but he did tell them that God believed in them. And God's belief in us, he wrote, really should elicit some response from us.

Roger began to need less morphine. He started to eat again. He told his friend later, "I think God has a plan for me right here in these letters!" Today, Roger's doctors call his recovery a miracle. If you ask Roger why he's still alive, he'll credit medical care as playing a significant role, and he's quick to give praise to his wife and family. But when Roger speaks from the heart, he will tell you the reason he's alive is because of those letters. He is alive because of gratitude.

I'm not sure that anything will re-wire your brain in a positive and healthy direction quite like being grateful. It is a decision you make, to start filling your mind with people and instances from your life for which you are grateful, to re-inforce it frequently in your thoughts, to develop the habit of gratitude.

It can be truly transforming to allow a sense of gratitude to become your mindset and attitude. A psychology professor conducted a study where one group of students kept a gratitude journal, a diary in which they recorded everything they were grateful for on a daily basis. Another group kept a complaint journal, which is just what it sounds like, a diary in which they recorded all of their complaints about what happened to them every day. Those who kept gratitude journals, this study reported, exercised more regularly, reported fewer physical symptoms, felt better about their lives as a whole, were more optimistic about the upcoming week, and were more likely to make progress toward important personal goals.

This is just the tip of the iceberg. Other studies reveal similar things. Studies on heart patients indicate that gratitude drives out toxic emotions of resentment, anger, and envy, and it may be associated with better long-term emotional and physical health in transplant recipients. Researchers also found that people who were grateful slept better, were less depressed and tired, and were more self-aware and confident, with lower risks of inflammation. Other studies show that gratitude promotes regular heart rhythms, rebalances hormones, reduces stress, increases relaxation, and promotes resistance to common illnesses.

In addition to heart health, gratitude has been linked to emotional well-being, lower levels of anxiety and depression, decreased panic attacks and phobias, and reduced risk of alcoholism and substance abuse. It has even been shown that grateful people live longer. Researchers found that thankful people live happier lives as well—they are more attentive to pleasure, are more contented, and retain good memories of the past easily.

Robert Emmons, one of the world's leading researchers on the subject, summarizes gratitude benefits as increased self-esteem, enhanced willpower, stronger relationships, deeper spirituality, boosted creativity, improved athletic and academic performance, and "having a unique ability to heal, energize, and change lives." Phew! All that from one simple, habitual choice we can consciously make every day: to be grateful.

Our minds—the thoughts and visions we place in them, what we direct ourselves to see, the way we wire our brains—have this tremendous effect on our health and well-being, and on our whole lives and future. Being grateful is one decision we can make to further us in the right direction on this journey. Being grateful is a decision we must make.

I heard about a woman who was 92. Her husband of 70 years had recently passed away, so she decided to move into a retirement center. She waited in the lobby patiently for some time. Finally, the director came and told her that her room was ready. As she stood up and maneuvered her walker toward the elevator, the director described the way her new room looked.

"I love it!" she said immediately, with the enthusiasm of an eight-year-old receiving a new puppy. "But you haven't even seen the room yet," said the director. "That doesn't matter," she said. "Happiness is something you decide on ahead of time. Whether I like the room or not doesn't depend on how the furniture is arranged. It all depends on how I arrange my mind, and I have already decided to love it. It's a decision I make every morning when I wake up. I can be happy or sad; I can be grateful or grumpy. I choose to see each day as a gift from God. I choose to be happy and grateful."

So can I. So can you!

Step Two

Do you believe your life ultimately consists of the vision and thoughts you choose for yourself? What specific thoughts are you choosing for yourself right now, today, this week? Can you think of five different people or things each day for which you are grateful? What objectives do you have—for your education, for your career, for your relationships, for your physical health? Strive for things that go beyond what comes easily. Can you picture yourself accomplishing these things? Can you see yourself there? What specific steps will you take to get there? What steps will you take to overcome or work through any obstacles or opposition?

3

DREAM BIG OR DREAM SMALL

Believe In The Power Of Doing It Now

Tightrope walker Charles Blondin, carrying his manager, Harry Colcord.

I have a friend who, in college and law school, had a girlfriend who he was mad about. They met and hit it off immediately and were a couple for almost five years. She was his first love, and they talked openly about how theirs was a relationship that would last forever. However, they felt they were too young and not quite ready for marriage.

As he graduated from law school, a professional opportunity opened up for him and he jumped at it. But it meant moving, and she wasn't ready to move her life and career at that point. So it was a long-distance relationship for a while, and they both struggled to keep their commitment to each other.

Finally, she broke it off. Well, he was devastated. They both were, but she saw more than he that they were growing apart and their lives were headed in different directions. He offered to move back, but she thought that was a mistake he would regret and hold against her.

There was one bold move he might make though, to save the relationship: he could fly back and show up at her apartment unannounced. In his mind, he would win her back and they would live happily ever after. It happened that way in the movies.

But the real world was very different, his new job was consuming and challenging, and when he confided his plan to a friend, he was advised not to go. "You'll be taking time you don't have away from work," he was told. "You'll have spent all that money on a last-minute fare. And it won't change a thing. You'll come back broke and even more heartbroken."

So, in the end, he didn't go, and before long the relationship was well and truly over. Eventually they lost track of each other. He was successful at what he did, got married, had children. But he always had this thought in the back of his mind: What might my life have been if I had gotten on that airplane?

Years later, they ran into each other and sat down for coffee. She was married too, with a child, and seemed content. At one point he told her that he had almost gotten on a plane and shown up at her apartment to try to win her back. With a slight tremor in her voice, she asked, "Why didn't you?"

Until my friend told me this, you would never have thought he lived with any disappointment of this sort. He seemed happy and deeply in love with his wife of many years. But as he spoke, you could see that he had lived with a sense of regret and continued to live with it, now into his fifties. It wasn't that he was pining away and miserable—that wasn't my read, anyway—but there would forever be a part of him that just couldn't stop wondering what might have been if he had gotten on that plane.

Her words, "Why didn't you?" just seemed to reverberate in his mind as if it were yesterday. This bold plan had been right there in his head: he could picture himself going, see the look on her face, imagine the happy reunion, the renewed commitment to each other, the plotting of plans for the future. It might have turned out that way.

Of course, it might have turned out exactly the opposite; he might have spent the night on the couch or in a hotel, frustrated and even sadder, counting the minutes until he could get on the expensive flight home. He might have been introduced to a new boyfriend she hadn't told him about. Or they might have reconciled and gotten back together, he might have moved back to be with her, married, had kids—and been unhappy over the long term, living with regret that he never got to pursue his dream job, wondering what other opportunities he'd missed, perhaps even getting divorced. There are lots of scenarios that could have turned this into a disaster.

The point is that he will never know. He never got on the plane, never took the chance, never made that one step necessary toward the fulfillment of his plan.

Which leads me to this question of you: Are there any airplanes you wish now that you had gotten on? Any opportunities that didn't come your way because you failed to reach out and grab it? Any chances you realize now were missed? Things might not have turned out all that differently in the end if you had gotten on, but there's that nagging suspicion that something really good might have come of it. And the thing is, you'll never know.

It's been said that most people don't regret the things they did in life nearly as much as the things they might have done but didn't. It has been suggested that hell is when God pulls aside the curtain of our lives in the end and shows us all we might have done and become, all he was calling us to, but we turned away and failed to grasp them.

But here, truly, is the bigger question: What will you do the next time there's a plane all gassed up and ready to go, waiting to see if you will come on board? Everything that has been said in the first two chapters of this book will be essentially worthless if you fail to do this one thing: take that step toward your goal, take that one action. You can practice steps one and two, speak positive and bold words to yourself, and visualize a dynamic future until the cows come home, but if you fail to take step three, which is to take some action toward that future, literally nothing will happen.

I live in Pittsburgh and grew up not far away in West Virginia. The Pirates have always been my baseball team, and as a boy, for me and nearly everyone here, Roberto Clemente was the man. My favorite story about him, though, happened before I was born, before I was even aware of what this great athlete could do. It was 1956, and the Pirates weren't a contender that year, struggling even to reach .500 for the season. But Clemente, in his sophomore year, was showing flashes of the brilliance to come in his career.

On this particular July day, the Pirates were behind 8-5, with the bases loaded and no one out in the bottom of the ninth. Clemente was at bat and on the first pitch, he hit it over the outfielder's head and against the wall in left field. While the ball was bouncing around in the outfield, the three base runners came home easily and the score was tied. Clemente, who was fast, was quickly at third base, and the coach put up the signal for him to hold there with a triple. But Clemente just kept going, barreling around third, almost knocking the coach over, and heading for home. He slid in just barely ahead of the tag to score the winning run.

It was the only documented walk-off, inside-the-park grand slam in history, and under the circumstances, Clemente was not ordered to pay the usual $25 fine for missing the signal from a base coach. He would later explain to the press in his heavy Dominican accent, "I think we have nothing to lose, as we got the score tied without my run, and I score, the game—she is over and we don't have to play no more tonight."

I love this story and have thought of it often, and I ask you to ponder this question: In what area of your life do you need to just go for it, take the chance, put everything on the line, everything you have into it? Maybe it's choosing a career or taking a job or going after that transfer or promotion. It might be swallowing your pride to take the initiative to reconcile a relationship, asking for help, giving a huge word of encouragement for someone who could really use it, letting go of a major disappointment or bitterness you've been holding onto, stepping out of your comfort zone to volunteer for an important project, being more generous with what you've been given in life.

The possibilities are endless, and the decision to go in pursuit of it might make all the difference in your life. It might be taking a risk, there might be something to lose by going for it, but there might be much more to lose if you don't.

So, what opportunity are you going to seize? There might be something right in front of you that's waiting for you to make the move. In fact, I'm convinced that if you look around thoroughly at your life, the people and things that are in it, there is at least one opportunity that you can seize right now or very soon. We all need to be asking ourselves more or less constantly: In what major place in my life am I going to round third, maybe ignoring someone else's signal to turn back, and head for home?

In a speech, President Theodore Roosevelt said these famous words, encapsulating this truth:

"It is not the critic who counts; not the man who points out how the strong man stumbles, or where the doer of deeds could have done them better. The credit belongs to the man who is actually in the arena, whose face is marred by dust and sweat and blood; who strives valiantly; who errs, who comes short again and again, because there is no effort without error and shortcoming; but who does actually strive to do the deeds; who knows great enthusiasms, the great devotions; who spends himself in a worthy cause; who at the best knows in the end the triumph of high achievement, and who at the worst, if he fails, at least fails while daring greatly, so that his place shall never be with those cold and timid souls who neither know victory or defeat."

I don't know about you, but I am energized every time I hear those words. In fact, I have accumulated quite a file of memorable, invigorating quotes that fire up the passion to do it—whatever it may be—and do it now. I especially love the short, pithy ones that are easy to remember, and there are these three that I seem to come back to time-after-time:

> It's only too late if you don't start now.
> The least important fact in life is the score at halftime.
> It's what you learn after you know it all that counts.

What I like about all three of these quotes is that they each are saying there is always room to learn and grow and move forward, it's never too late to get started, and there is always the possibility of taking some step, some action. So get moving!

Charles Blondin is a name you may recognize as perhaps the greatest tightrope walker in history. On June 30, 1859, before a stunned crowd of 100,000 excited onlookers, Blondin was the first person in history to cross Niagara Falls on a tightrope. He crossed 1,100 feet on a single three-inch-wide hemp cord, strung from 160 feet above the falls on one side to a spot 270 feet above the falls on the other. The breathless assembly watched him accomplish, step by step, a feat that simply seems unimaginable. But Blondin made the crossing easily, and he was just getting started.

In the years to come, the daring acrobat crossed again and again: on stilts, in a sack, on a bicycle, blindfolded. Once, he carried a small stove and cooked and ate an omelet on the rope in the middle of the falls.

And then there was the time he walked across the tightrope pushing a wheelbarrow. The story goes that when he reached the other side he yelled to the crowd, "I am the Great Blondin. Do you believe in me?"

Everyone yelled back, "We believe! We believe!" The thousands of voices were louder than the falls. Blondin yelled to them again, "Do you believe I can push a man across the falls in this wheelbarrow?" The crowd screamed back even louder, "We believe! We believe!"

So Blondin yelled to them once more, "Which one of you will climb into the wheelbarrow and go across the falls with me?" And the crowd suddenly grew absolutely still; no one said a word. One time, a man did step out of the crowd and climbed onto Blondin's back (not into a wheelbarrow) and went across the falls. It was later learned that it was Blondin's business manager, who had agreed to this ahead of time.

I'm not saying it's going to be easy to get into that wheelbarrow. To me, it is simply incomprehensible that Blondin did the things he did, much less that someone would climb into a wheelbarrow or get on his back. But isn't that the way it is in life? Often the things that turn out to be the most worthwhile and successful were once thought to be impossible.

I heard someone say that one of the widest gaps in our human experience is

An illustration of one of Charles Blondin's tightrope stunts.

the gap between what we say we want to be and our willingness to do what it takes to get there. We have to do more than just say that we want it, whatever it might be. We have to say we believe and train ourselves to actually believe; believe we can accomplish it, believe that it is worth the risk, believe that we must take some action, believe that we should do it now.

I'm fascinated by a man I'd never heard of until recently. By the time he had reached the age of 50, he had achieved essentially nothing that anyone would say was an accomplishment. He was what we would call an underachiever, someone with great promise that just never seemed to have been realized. Lack of any real ambition and issues of addiction had held him back.

But over the years, he'd written some poetry and a few short stories. A publisher got hold of his stuff somehow and approached him (he was in a pretty low level job at the time), and said he thought he could publish a novel by this man, if he had one.

He'd never written a novel before and didn't have anything to show him, but the publisher was convinced he could get one published. The only thing was that he would need it soon. Could this man commit himself to write a novel?

He later wrote about this critical turning point in his life, "I have one of two choices—stay where I am and go crazy . . . or stay out here and play at writing and starve."

He said, "I have decided to starve." So, he quit his job and started writing, and three weeks later he finished his novel, which was soon published. During the remainder of his life, he wrote five more novels, along with much poetry and other literary material. Altogether, his work sold over two million copies. So, it's not the Bible or Shakespeare, it's not *Harry Potter* or *Game of Thrones*, but it's a pretty good living for a writer, especially one who almost never published anything.

This man's name was Charles Bukowski. As I say, I'd never heard of him or his work before I heard his life story of struggle and success. Near the end of his life, he was interviewed and said, "We are to live our lives so well that Death will tremble to take us."

Now, I don't know what he meant—*he* might not have known exactly—but it sounds pretty great, doesn't it? What if we could grab hold of the sentiment of this, the spirit of it, and work it into our lives. Live your life so well that Death will tremble to take you. I think a lot of it has to do with simply taking that bold step forward, taking action, doing it. We might never have known of Charles Bukowski at all, if he had not decided to starve.

I would suggest to you that there are thousands, perhaps millions, of people who wanted to be writers, who told themselves that they could be writers, who saw themselves as writers, but who never actually became writers, because they didn't take that first step toward becoming a writer. They didn't sit down at a desk and start writing, they didn't send it in to a publisher, they didn't send it in to a second publisher if it was rejected the first time, or a third, whatever it took.

There are all kinds of people, I am convinced, in all kinds of vocations and work, who never made the kind of mark they always wanted to—perhaps as a nurse, or a teacher, an artist, a doctor, a research scientist, a police officer, a firefighter—because they did not take the first concrete step toward their dream. It always seemed too difficult, too much work, too expensive, too far beyond what others expected of them.

Too many of us die, as someone has described it, with the music still in us, without attempt, without trying to rise to the challenge, without taking that first step. The poet Rabindranath Tagore wrote these affecting lines: "The song I came to sing remains unsung to this day. I have spent my days in stringing and unstringing my instrument. The time has not come true, the words have not been rightly set; only there is the agony of wishing in my heart."

Do you remember the movie *Dead Poets Society*? Robin Williams made a deep impression on me as the dynamic teacher at an exclusive New England boys' school in the late 1950s. He was always trying to get the boys to think outside the box and think for themselves.

In one memorable scene, he takes them into the hall where all the trophies are kept in display cases to recognize the school's success in athletics. Pictures of the teams sit beside the trophies on the shelves. Williams has his students look at the pictures of those boys from the teams of long ago, to step up close and see their faces.

"They're not that different from you, are they?" he says. "Same haircuts, full of hormones, just like you. Invincible, just like you feel. The world is their oyster. They believe they're destined for great things, just like many of you. Their eyes are full of hope, just like you. Did they wait until it was too late to make from their lives even one iota of what they were capable? Because you see, gentlemen, these boys are now fertilizing daffodils." He goes on, "But if you listen real close, you can hear them whisper their legacy to you." He has them lean in. "Go on, listen, do you hear it?"

And then he says in a ghostlike whisper, trying to make it sound like it is coming to them from down through the ages, "Carpe. Carpe diem. Seize the day, boys. Make your lives extraordinary!"

His words remind me of that great quote of George Bernard Shaw: "I want to be thoroughly used up when I die, for the harder I work, the more I live. Life is no 'brief candle' to me. It is a sort of splendid torch which I have got hold of for a moment, and I want to make it burn as brightly as possible before handing it on to the future generations."

Do you want to make your life extraordinary? Do you really? You're not just saying that because you think that's what I want to hear, right? Do you want to make of it a sort of splendid torch? Then you really do need to take some action toward that. An extraordinary life won't just come to you. You must look for those opportunities to move forward. Take that first step. It really is the only way to reveal whether the pursuit of the dream you have in your mind is the right one for you or whether you might need to develop a different dream because your life as a splendid torch lies elsewhere.

W. Clement Stone was an executive in the insurance business who experienced huge success. He would start each morning by having his team say out loud, "Do it now. Do it now." They would repeat this phrase 50 times and then be ready to attack each day. Can you imagine, after the accumulation of days and months and years of saying these words 50 times each day, that any member of his team would not be ready to pounce on every opportunity that presented itself to them right then and there?

The same can be true for you.

So often, especially when we are younger, we think we have all the time in the world; there's no hurry, there's always tomorrow. It is such an undermining concept because it is true, there is always tomorrow. It's a fact that's hard to argue with. If you would indeed get started tomorrow, you've only lost one day, which isn't that big of a deal in the long run; you still have so much time to accomplish your plans. Tomorrow will do just fine as a beginning.

The problem is that 24 hours later it becomes today all over again, and once more there is always a tomorrow. Indeed, there is always a tomorrow ahead of you that seems limitless. Until, of course, one day you do run abruptly up against the limit. And I'm not just talking about death either, although that is the final end of all of our tomorrows. I'm saying that opportunities do run their course at some point, options and alternatives do expire.

My friend did have a few tomorrows to make his decision as to whether or not to get on that airplane, but finally she, and he too, had gotten on with life and there was no more plane waiting to be boarded and taken for a ride to what a different life might have offered.

Sir Walter Scott's last entry in his diary was apparently, "Tomorrow I will…" Now he may have accomplished quite a lot during his lifetime, but if there was even one iota of what he put off that he could have done today, there is at least some diminishment of the fullness of life he could have experienced.

Let me make it absolutely clear in words that you can say to yourself each day: Do it now. Take action. Seize the day. Get in that wheelbarrow. Get on that airplane. Starve if you must, but do it now! The German writer Johann Goethe put it much more poetically: "Whatever you can do, or dream you can, begin it; boldness has genius, power and magic in it."

Deion Sanders inspired the Dallas Cowboys with a saying: "The play doesn't care who makes it."

Take that step. It is not necessarily trying to accomplish something big all at once that counts; it is being willing to take that first step, to travel step-by-step toward your goal, that makes all the difference. Studies have shown that we over-estimate our willpower to make big changes in our lives. We have this big goal for ourselves; we say to ourselves that we're going to lose weight, for example. And then we are frustrated when after a week or a month or a year we weigh the same as we did when we started (or even more!).

But if we take one concrete step—turn down that first chocolate chip cookie, go to the gym, take a walk—we begin to work toward our goal. Those who set a big goal but have no specific ways of getting there, think it's just a matter of having a strong willpower, or that it's going to be easy, recent research has shown, have a lot more difficulty getting to their goal.

Those who are most likely to achieve their goal went into it with the belief that it was going to be harder than anyone else could anticipate. The ones who went into it thinking, "This is going to be tough," got the goal much more often than the people who went into it thinking, "This will be easy, I can do this no problem."

The reason seems to be that if we think it's going to be hard, we are more realistic about what we are facing, and we begin to try and understand what it will take and what we must do, step by step, to achieve it.

As a result, it is important for us to take small steps. Martin Luther King Jr. said once about dreams and visions, "Real faith is taking the steps up the stair-case, one at a time, even though you don't know where the staircase is headed."

A few years ago, when I was working with the Dallas Cowboys, there was a phrase that was popular with the players that came from retired NFL player Deion Sanders: "The play doesn't care who makes it."

He would say it all the time, and I didn't understand at first just what he was saying, but here's what he meant. So many ballplayers in the NFL say things like, "I'm going to make a play," or, "On this down, I'm going to do something big." And what they usually end up doing is blowing it, giving up a long pass, dropping the ball, or throwing an interception.

They were saying, "I've got to do something big right now," and it was too much pressure, what they were trying to do in a single play was simply too big.

What Deion was saying was just go do your job right now, go do your pro-cess, take the actions you need to take to be the player you want to be, because you never know when the play is going to come to you. Don't go out and say, "I have to do something huge right now." No, do your job right now and, in time, the play will come to you.

There was a wide receiver Deion was teaching this to when I was down there. During the first quarter of one game, he didn't get a single pass, but he just kept doing his pass patterns and running hard. In the second quarter, he didn't get a pass, but he kept working hard and following his routine. In the third quarter, he caught a 70-yard bomb for a touchdown! And he quoted what Deion had taught him, "The play doesn't care who makes it."

We have to keep going and going, working hard, taking each step toward the goal, even though we don't know when the goal will be revealed, and then the play will come to us. Even if we don't know where the staircase goes, just take a step, then the next, and then the one after that.

Do small things. Sometimes I tell people, "Dream small, don't dream big." Dream small, meaning do the small things, take the small steps, and these will turn into the big things and the achieving of that goal. As you do the small things, all of a sudden the touchdown, the trophy, the medal will show up. But in doing the small things, you're showing that you have faith even if there are not big rewards, at least not immediately. Mother Teresa was often quoted as saying, "We can do no great thing, only small things with great love."

I heard someone talking about the secret of instant success, and he said that the secret is usually years and years of hard work. Oh sure, some people do just happen into success without all that much effort, but for most it is a lot of hard, determined work to win a Super Bowl or write a book or become a teacher or achieve your financial goals. Others may only notice you when you arrive, so to them it may seem like you have achieved something more or less instantly. Only you know how much has gone into it, only you understand how difficult it was to take that first step, to take it step by step.

I often think of Joshua as he led the Israelites through the Jordan River and into the Promised Land. I wonder if he was at all intimidated to know that this journey would remind the people of the crossing that had been made with Moses through the Red Sea. The Red Sea crossing had truly been a miraculous spectacle they would always remember: Moses had stretched forth his arms and lifted up his staff, and the Red Sea had parted.

But the crossing of the Jordan River would not happen in quite so dramatic a fashion. Joshua was instructed that the priests carrying the ark of the covenant would be required to first go into the river and stand there. This must have been a daunting task, since they were stepping into a swiftly moving stream rather than walking on dry land with the water already parted as in Moses' time. I have been to Israel and visited the Jordan River. I don't know if scholars have tried to identify exactly where the Israelites might have crossed, but depending on the season, the current can move along quite briskly.

There was a big faith that was revealed with that first small step. But when the priests carrying the ark of the covenant stepped into the Jordan and stood there, we're told that the water stopped flowing and piled up as if someone had built a dam across the river. It was then that the people walked across to the Promised Land.

One small step can make all the difference. There is a simple little book that was published recently that makes this point brilliantly. In fact, it's contained in the book title and sub-title: *Make Your Bed: Little Things that Can Change Your Life . . . and Maybe the World.* It was written by retired four-star Admiral William H. McRaven, who, as commander of the Joint Special Operations Command, is credited with organizing and overseeing the special operations raid that led to the death of Osama bin Laden.

Of the ten little things he writes about, the first and (to him) most important is to make your bed. Experience the lift and satisfaction that comes from completing a task as you begin the day. "It will give a small sense of pride and it will encourage you to do another task and another and another. By the end of the day, that one task completed will have turned into many tasks completed. Making your bed will also reinforce the fact that little things matter."

Now, maybe for you that first task of the day is not to make your bed. I have read this book twice and love it and talk about it to anyone who will listen, and I still don't make mine. But there's a principle here that is absolutely indispensable.

What one thing can you do each morning that will set the tone for the day, that will be a small step in the right direction, provide some lift and satisfaction as you begin? Maybe for you it's physical: take a walk, get your 10,000 steps in, do something to work up a sweat, or eat a healthy breakfast. All of these things, and more, will create the right mood for your life for the day ahead.

Or maybe your start to the day is on a more spiritual plane. "Make your bed" means begin with prayer, meditation, or reading the Bible or other poetic or devotional material that captures an almost boundless and otherworldly quality that contrasts with what you will encounter in your real world that day. Don't immediately look at the news or see who has emailed or texted. Don't jump right into the middle of the circumstances you will face all the rest of the day. Set a timeless sense and eternal quality to the tone and atmosphere of your life that will give you a different perspective throughout the day and remind you of what is truly significant. Be bold here because this is a big one—be the thermostat every morning as you begin, not the thermometer.

U.S. Navy Admiral William H. McRaven's book, *Make Your Bed*, focuses on how small actions can help make major life changes.

Set the tone for your day by taking that first step of real meaning each morning. Set the tone for your life by being ready when each opportunity presents itself to seize on it, take action, hold nothing back. Believe in the power of doing it now.

I heard of this young woman who had the desire to be a missionary to China. This was many years ago when the country was just beginning to open up to foreigners, particularly Westerners, who wanted to come and share the Good News of Jesus Christ with the Chinese people. This young woman felt that God was calling her to go, and she was committed to go. She had gone through the whole process that was required by the missionary society, she'd been interviewed and accepted, taken language courses, and gone through all the orientation. She was ready to go, she kept telling everyone, she kept telling herself.

And yet somehow, she *wasn't* quite ready. She was afraid. She had been called, of that she was sure. But in so many other ways she was still so unsure. Her life was going to be so different. Was she really going to go through with it?

One night, she had a dream. She was out in the middle of the ocean and walking to China. At first, it was such a scary experience; there was water all around and she felt that she could submerge and drown at any moment. But she kept walking, and she began to notice that as she took each step, a plank or board would emerge out of the water and support her foot. There was nothing there as she looked ahead of her, only water, but as she took each step, just as she was about to place her foot down right into the water, a plank would emerge out of the depths to support her foot. The planks kept appearing to support her every step of the way.

The next day she was ready to go and soon departed for what turned out to be a long and productive career as a missionary to China. Being willing to take that first step, that one small step, step-after-step, with God's guidance (as we see here and we'll see more fully developed in a later chapter), with the encouragement of others (as we'll also see in a later chapter), or with a singular determination that is all our own. Take that step; there is such boldness in each step.

Step Three

What dreams or goals do you have for your life? Write them out, state them specifically to yourself. What is the first bold step you must take toward that dream or goal? Believe in the power of doing it now and take that step. What is the next step? Take that step, and the next, and the next. What is the one thing you must do each morning to set the proper tone and quality for the day ahead and for your life? Do that thing each day without fail.

4 POSITION OR DISPOSITION

Believe in Your Own Resilience

Tiger Woods at the 2019 U.S. Open.

When I was 58 years old, paramedics carried me out of my house on a stretcher, put me in an ambulance, and took me to the hospital. I'd just had a heart attack.

They told me I missed dying by two minutes.

I called in my wife and children and told them goodbye. Honestly, I had more peace about this than I would have thought possible before it happened. I had a deep sense of faith and hope. What came over me was that soon I was going to be with my parents again and other family members and friends who had passed on.

But, of course, there was a big part of me that wanted to live, too. My daughter and son weren't all grown up yet, and I wanted to see them go to college, get married, and have children of their own. There were still things I wanted to accomplish in my career as a speaker and writer.

In a way, this heart attack was inevitable. Although I'd always exercised and eaten pretty well, my genetic makeup made me vulnerable. My mother was one of 12 children and my father one of 8; out of those 20, 19 died of heart disease. My slightly older sister, petite and fit, had quadruple bypass surgery not long before this chapter was written. So we came by our health problems honestly, as part of a family line with a history of heart disease. In a very real sense, I was in a position where there was essentially nothing I could do. "His time was up," it would have said on my tombstone if I had died.

But I didn't die. I'm still alive and want to be even more fully alive than ever as a result of my experience. I'm writing this book, in part, because I've learned some things about life and about myself as a result of this heart attack.

On my first Sunday back in church after my stay in the hospital, my friend and pastor (now my co-author) used an illustration that caught my attention right away. He talked about a golf course in Calcutta, India, that had been built by the British during colonial days.

It had this unique obstacle that the builders just hadn't anticipated. They realized there were monkeys around when they surveyed the area but hadn't envisioned what that might mean for the course. The monkeys had largely disappeared during construction, but when it was completed, they showed back up. They would drop down out of the trees and grab the golf balls, play with them, and throw them here and there.

Well, of course, the British tried to control the monkeys. First, they built fences around the fairways and around the greens. But a fence is no match for a determined monkey, and they still got in.

So they tried to lure them away with food and shiny objects. But the monkeys would not be lured away; it was much more fun to watch the human beings go wild when their little golf balls were disturbed.

Then they tried to trap the monkeys and take them away. But for every monkey that was trapped and taken away, it seemed like another monkey, or even another six, would show up.

So finally, they came up with a novel new ground rule, which was absolutely unique to this golf course. The rule: "Play the ball where the monkey drops it." The monkey was going to be part of the game, so you might as well get used to that.

Sometimes the monkeys would help you; they might pick up a bad shot and drop it on the green. But most of the time, the monkeys were going to hurt your play. They might pick up a good shot, maybe the best shot of your life, and throw it anywhere, drop it in any direction, even into the rough. The golfers had to learn to play the ball where the monkey dropped it.

My pastor and friend said that day that our lives can be like this; we have to live our lives the way they come, the way whatever forces are out there seem to throw them and drop them, in whatever rough places we might find ourselves. I sat in my seat and nodded knowingly.

A golf course in Goa, India

The question I was asking myself in those days after my heart attack was how I was going to live my life now that the monkey had dropped the ball in a certain direction. Ralph Waldo Emerson once said we are not responsible for what happens to us, but we are responsible for the way we behave when things do happen. Someone else has said, "We don't have the luxury of choosing our circumstances, but we can always choose our attitude."

What was my responsibility now to the circumstances that had happened to me? What attitude was I going to choose?

Similar to these quotes, there was a phrase that I had used occasionally beforehand, but now I began to use it all the time: "That didn't happen *to* me, that happened *for* me." There was something to be gained from my experience, something to be learned. My position in life was heart attack victim, but my disposition was going to be something else entirely, something of my own choosing. I was going to try my best to be the thermostat, not the thermometer, from now on.

I remember a friend telling me quite a while ago that he had gone through a serious illness, one that could be fatal, but he had survived and healed. Then he said that it had been a privilege to go through that illness, and it had been a privilege to recover from it. I knew what he meant in a vague sort of way back when he first told me, but I know exactly what he meant now.

To learn more about yourself, to grow, to become a deeper and better person as a result of it, this was truly a privilege that I was going to try to make the most of. "We find out who we really are when the earthquake hits," is how someone else expressed it.

What I can say is that the year after my heart attack was the best year of my life. I like to say it was the best year in the history of years. I made sure of this. I chose it—every day. I feel like I truly live every day. I try to be more conscious of the gratitude I have for each day, for each person in my day and for everything that happens during the day. My life was taken from me and it was given back.

In fact, I would almost wish for you that you could have a heart attack, that your life could be taken away and then given back to you.

What I learned in that year can be summed up in one word: ownership. Here is another phrase I say to myself and speak into my life now: "The best year of my life will be the year I take ownership of every problem in my life."

I took ownership of what happened. I went to the Cleveland Clinic, and got on something called the Ornish Reversal Diet. It's a diet designed to reverse heart disease. I'm a total vegan now. I run sprints every day. I run and do other types of HIIT (high intensity interval training) for strength and conditioning.

And I meditate. This may be the single most important thing. What I do often is read the Psalms. I spend a lot of time on the 23rd Psalm. I go through very slowly.

When I get to the part that says, "My cup runneth over," I sit and see all the things and people that have blessed my life, all the ways my life runs over with blessing. When I read, "He maketh me to lie down in green pastures; he leadeth me beside the still waters. He restoreth my soul . . .," I literally visualize laying down in lush, green pastures, and he, God, is the one there directing me to lay down in a place of beauty and solace and peace. It is as though I am experiencing the restoration of my very soul.

When they told me at the Cleveland Clinic that no one needs to die from heart disease, I believed them. When they said, "Do this and take ownership and you'll live a long time," I did just that. It's changed the way I take ownership of other things in my life, too.

I wanted the door handle to be on my side of the door; in other words, I wanted to take more control over my life in every way possible, rather than let my circumstances dictate what my life will be. I realize more than ever that my time is my wealth, and I enjoy every day. I live every day. I'm thankful at a deep level every day. I've never seen this day before; it's a brand-new day.

Nick Saban, head coach of the University of Alabama football team, is a good friend of mine and called me in the hospital when he heard about my heart attack. Trying, I guess, to make me feel better somehow, he told me about his father who died of a heart attack at 44 years old. "There's nothing you can do," he said. "It's genetic."

Later, he sent me a box of chocolates as a get-well present. I called him back and said, "Are you trying to kill me or something?" It was a joke, but it was no joking matter.

Taking ownership of my health meant that I wasn't going to be able to eat that chocolate. I refused to do what I had mostly done before, what most people did, I suppose, which was to eat that kind of thing and then say there was nothing I could do about my health. My situation or position was not inevitable, it would not have the final word.

It would be my disposition in the face of my heart attack, the choices and decisions I would make from here on out, that would have the most say over my outcome and future. I would take responsibility for what had happened to me. I did not choose my circumstances, but I would choose my attitude.

I love stories of children who rise to the occasion in heroic ways. For example, there was one little girl who had a very serious illness, but she didn't seem to let it derail her plans to continue to explore life, to learn and grow. She was very active, too active apparently for one adult who was a friend of the family and wanted to protect her. She almost scolded the little girl once when she saw her playing too vigorously: "You're going to have to take it easy. Don't you know that you have a very serious illness? Don't you know that this will color your whole life?"

And the little girl, not only bravely but maturely, I think, responded, "I know it will color my life, but I'm going to choose what color that will be!"

Another precocious little boy was born without a hand. From a young age, he realized that he was different from other boys and girls, but he participated as energetically as any of the other children. He even learned to play the outfield in baseball, catching the ball in the mitt with his one good hand, then quickly switching the mitt under his arm and pulling the ball out of the mitt with the hand that had just caught it, and throwing it into the infield with strength and accuracy.

He was very good and everyone who saw him for the first time always marveled at what he could do. One man said to him one day, "Hey kid, you're pretty good for someone who has a handicap." The little boy looked at him with a kind of bewildered expression, and said innocently, "I don't have a handicap. I just don't have a hand." Surely such ownership of one's problems so early on will develop habits of resilience that will enable this boy to see that so much of the difficulties and adversities of life happen for you, not to you.

And I love stories of older people who don't let their age or infirmity stop them from a full and creative life, right up to the end. My favorite is French Impressionist painter Auguste Renoir, who was essentially confined to his home for the last ten years or so of his life because of progressively worsening rheumatoid arthritis. It affected his hands more than anything.

They became severely deformed, to the point that he had to change his painting technique. He was able to grasp a paintbrush, but an assistant had to place it in his hand, which was essentially a rigid, vicelike claw. The arthritis caused a great deal of pain, especially as he was painting. If you search his name on YouTube, one of the first things that comes up is a three-minute video of him painting during these later years.

One of his best friends, especially through these difficult years, was another Impressionist painter, Henri Matisse, who was much younger and considered Renoir an indispensable mentor. Matisse visited him almost daily, apparently.

During one visit, as he watched the elder painter work at his art, fighting torturous pain with his deformed hands as he performed each brushstroke, Matisse

"Self-portrait" (1910), a later work by Auguste Renoir.

exclaimed, "Auguste, why do you continue to paint when you are in such agony?" And Renoir replied, "The pain passes, but the beauty remains."

Another famous artist also experienced his most difficult times during his last years. The experience of Rembrandt van Rijn was principally one of the decline in his financial fortunes. He lived beyond his means, buying lavish paintings, statues, prints, and other rarities, among other things. At one point, he sold most of these well below what he had paid for them in order to narrowly avoid bankruptcy. He had to sell his opulent home in a fashionable neighborhood and move to a very modest home.

When he died, he was buried as a poor man in an unknown grave along with others, somewhere under a tombstone that belonged to the church. After 20 years, all of the remains, including his, were taken away and destroyed, as was customary with the remains of poor people of the time.

Think of the stress of being wealthy and famous at an early stage of one's life, having it all, and then losing it all and coming to this kind of an end. And yet, most art historians agree that Rembrandt's finest paintings belong to these difficult final years. A brilliance continued to shine through. In fact, the brilliance shone through all the more clearly throughout, and one wonders if it was as a result of, these troubling times.

Illness can strike at any time. The monkey will sometimes drop the ball in the most devastating of places. There can be pain, loss, failure, poverty, natural disaster, and human-made disaster. Any of these things can come in and wreck your life at just about any time. And sometimes, as in Rembrandt's case, we can, in part, do it to ourselves.

And yet, there is a constant supply of stories of those who have overcome these kinds of obstacles—and much more. There are many instances of people growing healthier and stronger, becoming more determined, creating a beauty and a meaning that might not have been realized had circumstances not forced them to take more ownership of their difficulties and their lives.

That didn't happen *to* them, whatever it is; it happened *for* them. One might think that their circumstances meant they were in a position of being diminished and devalued. But their disposition in the midst of those circumstances showed them to be sturdy and thriving.

I think it must have been just this kind of disposition that Paul had in mind when he said, "We often suffer, but we are never crushed. Even when we don't know what to do, we never give up. In times of trouble, God is with us, and when we are knocked down, we get up again" (II Corinthians 4:8-9). What seems like a disaster can be just the beginning of something really worthwhile.

I have spent a lot of time working with the University of Alabama football team and traveling throughout the state. At one point, someone took me to the little town of Enterprise in southern Alabama, where there is a very unique monument right in the middle of town.

I have to tell you that it is one of the ugliest statues I think I've ever seen. But the people there love it, and as they told me about it, I began to, if not love it, at least appreciate it and respect and admire the people who have lived there. The year was 1915 and the boll weevil, an insect native to Mexico, appeared for the first time in Alabama. Quickly, it became devastating to the main crop of the state, cotton. Soon farmers were losing their whole crops to this ravenous insect and were facing financial ruin. The leaders of one small town, Enterprise, rather than seeing this as a disaster, saw it as an opportunity and convinced farmers to try a different crop, peanuts.

Indebted farmers in the area began to switch to the new crop, and with one harvest, many of them paid off all their debts, with some left over. The farming of peanuts soon became more profitable than cotton had ever been.

A monument to the boll weevil was built in 1919 as a tribute to how something disastrous can be a catalyst for change, and a reminder of how the people of Enterprise adjusted in the face of adversity. The statue of a Greek goddess stands in the middle of town holding a boll weevil. It's ugly, as I say, and also beautiful because of what it represents. The plaque that is posted nearby says simply, "In profound appreciation of the Boll Weevil and what it has done as the herald of prosperity this monument was erected by the citizens of Enterprise, Coffee County, Alabama."

When something happens to us, we can see it as a danger that is lurking there ahead of us, as a potential disaster. Or, we can see it as an opportunity to try something new, to go in a different direction, to think in a new way.

Various people have expressed it like this, that disappointments and difficulties can make us bitter or better, they can create in us something hard or hopeful, they can be a stumbling block or a stepping stone.

Let me tell you about a man whose whole life seemed to consist of one defeat or disappointment after another. It started at a young age; in fact, it's hard to see that he had any real chance in life at all. He was born into extreme poverty, and at age seven he and his parents were forced out of their home. His mother died when he was nine, and as

The Boll Weevil Monument in Enterprise, Alabama.

a result, he never finished grade school and never went to high school or college.

At 23, he tried to start a business, but it failed. He then tried politics, running for a lower-level office, and lost. Then he lost his job. At 24, he borrowed money to start another business, but it failed too, and he spent the next 17 years trying to pay off the debt. At 26, he got engaged, but his fiancée died before the wedding. At 27, he had a total nervous breakdown and for six months did almost nothing.

At 29, he tried politics again, and lost his first campaign for the state legislature, before winning the next election and serving four terms. Next he ran for Congress, and once again he lost. It was at some point during these years that he wrote to a friend, "I am now the most miserable man living. If what I feel were equally distributed to the whole human family, there would not be one cheerful face on earth." It was also during this time that he did get married, but it was never a happy marriage.

At the age of 37, he ran for Congress and actually won a two-year term. But two years later he chose not to run for re-election and sought a position with the General Land Office, for which he was rejected.

Unbelievably, I think, given all of his past failures, when he was 45, he ran for the U.S. Senate and lost. Two years later he sought to be his party's nominee for vice president, but he was not selected. Two years after that, he ran for the Senate again, but again he was defeated.

I have to pause here and ask: How many of us would have given up by now? How much defeat and disappointment and failure is one person expected to endure? This man did have some limited success over the course of his life; he was a respected professional, a self-made lawyer. He had a personality that people genuinely liked. Although he was sometimes grim and suffered with what was then called "melancholy," which we would probably call today "depression," he could be full of mirth and keep people spellbound with his tall tales. But so much of his life was characterized by unfulfilled dreams and unrealized determination. His experience was of one demoralizing, heartbreaking, sometimes tragic episode after another.

And yet, to continue with the story of this man's life, two years after he lost his bid for the Senate, at the age of 51, Abraham Lincoln ran for and was elected to the office of president of the United States. He has been described as the most inexperienced and least prepared person ever to hold this office.

Historians have generally seen him as not really ready for the position he was taking on. And yet he was perhaps our greatest president because, as one historian argues, "he had this tremendous capacity for personal growth." It was not his position that made him great, it was his disposition. He was able not just to get through the setbacks and failures and suffering, but to use them as periods of insight and learning and growth. These episodes led to a greater depth of being, a greater understanding and wisdom and maturity, a broadening and strengthening of his character, which would be just the preparation needed for the long and bloody struggle for national unity that lay ahead.

There is a long list of so many who have faced incredible, seemingly insurmountable odds and have overcome, not just in spite of, but because of their suffering and adversity, because of the strength and depth they gained in the process. Here are just a few of the names:

Lock him in a prison cell, beat him, and shipwreck him, and you have the apostle Paul.

Deafen him, and you have a Ludwig van Beethoven.

Cripple him, and you have a brilliant novelist and poet—Sir Walter Scott.

Bury him in the snows of Valley Forge following defeat after defeat, and you have a George Washington.

Burn him so severely at the age of three that doctors say he'll never walk again, and you have a Glenn Cunningham—the man who set the world's one-mile record in 1934.

Call him a slow learner, label him "retarded," and write him off as uneducable, and you have an Albert Einstein.

Strike him down with polio, and he becomes a Franklin D. Roosevelt.

Have him or her born black in a society filled with racial prejudice and discrimination, and you have a Harriet Tubman, Booker T. Washington, George Washington Carver, Marian Anderson, Rosa Parks, or Martin Luther King Jr.

Subject him to torture in a Japanese prison camp for more than three years, and you have a Louis Zamperini.

Have him born of parents who survived a Nazi concentration camp, paralyze him from the waist down when he is four, and you have the concert violinist Itzhak Perlman.

I am particularly fascinated by the final name on this list. A famous legend about Itzhak Perlman's concert at Lincoln Center with the New York Philharmonic Orchestra reveals the true resilience of this man, who has been called the greatest violinist of our age.

Right in the middle of the piece he was playing, one of the strings on his violin broke. You could hear the snap of it throughout the auditorium. The conductor looked over to see if they should stop playing; did Perlman want to take a break to fix his violin? But Perlman signaled for him to continue.

A music critic who witnessed this event wrote about it this way: "I know that it's impossible to play a symphonic work with just three strings. I know that and you know that, but that night Itzhak Perlman refused to know that. You could see him up there modulating, changing, re-composing the piece in his head."

When he finished, at first there was just this awesome, stunned silence throughout the auditorium. But then everyone was on his or her feet, clapping and screaming and cheering for this incredible performance. When the crowd quieted down, Perlman very modestly said, "You know, sometimes it is the artist's opportunity to find out how much music you can still make with what you have left."

In each one of us there is a capacity for resilience, this ability to bounce back from adversity, the emotional toughness and strength of purpose to continue despite the obstacles. It is the ability to grow and build character and think in a new way when adversity comes, to follow a different direction if necessary. It is having a toughness about you, the grit to keep moving forward and never give up, the disposition to see everything as an opportunity. It is training yourself to see that something didn't happen to you, it happened for you. It is taking ownership of your problems and of your life.

Is there something you are in the midst of? Something you're facing? It would be the rare person whose life isn't involved in some challenge or difficulty.

I still remember the person who told me once that everyone is facing some problem; either you are in the midst of a problem right now, or you are just going into one or just coming out of one. This may be overstating it a bit; we aren't all facing something fatal or ruinous.

But whether it is something potentially devastating or something that only presents a challenge, something that is testing you, how will you respond? How will you take ownership of your problem? How will you see it as something that isn't happening to you, but something that is happening for you? What will you choose in response to those circumstances? Does your situation put you in a bad position, or does it give you the opportunity to develop a disposition of boldness and determination and resilience?

Perhaps the comeback story of 2019 is that of Tiger Woods. When he broke onto the professional golfing scene in 1996, no one had quite seen anything like him. After a successful junior amateur and college career, Tiger turned pro at 20 in 1996, and within a year he was the number one player in the world, the fastest ascent to that ranking in history.

Between 1997 and 2008, he won four Masters Tournaments and 14 Majors in all, second only to Jack Nicklaus. He won the 2000 U.S. Open with a record

15 strokes under par, ten strokes ahead of the next place finisher, in what *Sports Illustrated* called "the greatest performance in golf history."

I'll never forget watching him on that last day of play. The winner had long since been decided, but even without any competition between the top two players, I was transfixed watching this brilliant young man swing his clubs flawlessly and stalk the course with a relentlessness that was simply thrilling.

For over a decade, except for a few weeks, he was ranked as the number one player in the world. *Forbes* magazine claimed in 2009 that he was the world's first professional athlete to earn over a billion dollars in his career. At the age of 33, he was essentially considered the greatest golfer of all-time. He had it all. It is hard to say enough about this young man and all his accomplishments.

Then, his life began to unravel. His father had died in 2006, which left him somewhat unmoored from not only the biggest motivational force behind his participation in golf, but the greatest influence in his life. In November 2009, his wife chased him out of their home with a golf club after learning that he'd been unfaithful. She had thrown his phone at him, chipping his tooth, and scratched his face before grabbing a club and pursuing him out the door. He got into his Cadillac Escalade but hit a fire hydrant before smashing into a tree. Tiger wound up lying in the street, unconscious and bloody.

Tiger later admitted to being a sex addict, having had numerous mistresses and affairs, and the sordid news about all this splashed across the headlines and plunged the superstar into scandal. He entered rehab, but his relationship with his wife, the mother of his two children, never recovered, and they divorced the next year. We talked earlier about how sometimes we can do it to ourselves, we can be our own worst enemies. Some of the positions in which we find ourselves can be places where we have put ourselves.

In the ensuing years, Tiger played well, winning a few tournaments but no Majors. He was out of the game from time-to-time with back pain and four surgeries within five years. The worst of these was in April 2017. Here is how he described the pain in his back in an interview: "For the better part of four to six months, I had to be helped out of bed every day. And there were some days where you'd help me and I couldn't stand up. I'd have to either just fall to the floor or just stay in bed."

A month later, as he was recovering from the surgery and on pain medication, Tiger made headlines again off the golf course. He was found asleep at the wheel of his Mercedes near his mansion in Jupiter, Florida, and failed a sobriety test (though no alcohol was found in his system). He later pleaded guilty to reckless driving. I remember the mugshot of Tiger that somehow leaked to the press.

Tiger Woods has made a comeback in the professional golf world, winning his fifth Masters in 2019.

There he was, disheveled, bleary, unfocused, a criminal caricature of his former, dashing self.

I've detailed so much of Tiger's life for a couple of reasons. First, there simply is a lot to tell if you want to get a full picture of his ups and downs. But more than that, you and I are going to have some ups and downs in our lives. They may not be lived out nearly as publicly as his were, but to you, they may feel just as devastatingly low. Like all the stories of people in this chapter, including my own, there is always the opportunity to come back, to learn, to grow, to get better, to be hopeful, to choose to see that this didn't happen to you, it happened for you.

And to complete his redemption story, on April 14, 2019, Tiger Woods came from behind and won his fifth Masters, and 15th Major, tournament. In one interview afterward, he talked about being lucky to be playing again after all that has transpired and about being as patient as he's been in a long time, in control of his emotions and of his shots.

He said, "I was just trying to plod my way across the golf course all day. Plod my way around." Taking it step by step, in other words, working hard, playing his game, until, "All of a sudden, I had the lead."

In another interview, he saw his come-from-behind victory in a larger context beyond golf, that of overcoming adversity in life. "No one's perfect," he admitted. "Everyone is dealt cards in their life, there are obstacles we all have to overcome. Some are different than others. I certainly have had my obstacles that I've had to try and overcome, and to fight, to get back up, and to know that this is all not done alone, I've had a fantastic group of people around me, and their love and support have helped." He concluded, "I had to battle to get back to this point. It feels good."

Step Four

Is there any negative thing that you feel has happened to you? Repeat to yourself: This didn't happen to me, this happened for me. List all the benefits that have come from this. Be specific. Write them down. List as many as you can. Look at the list daily. Think about what it means to take ownership of your problems and ownership of your life. Write down three practices you will do to take ownership. Do these three practices every day.

5

INTEND OR DECIDE

Believe In Your Own Purpose

Two days after my 60th birthday, I picked up a little book by Anne Lamott and read these words: "What if you wake up at 60 and realize that you forgot to wake up, and you never became the person you were born to be, and now your hair is falling out?"

I had actually read her book, *Stitches: A Handbook on Meaning, Hope and Repair*, several years before, and so I must have read those words, but they hadn't had much of an effect on me at the time. But that day, as I read them, I paused and thought about what she was asking. Maybe it was because my hair was now starting to fall out just a bit, in a place or two. Or was it simply the coincidence of reading about waking up to the meaning of life at 60 when I had just turned that age? Whatever it was, I felt wide awake now, and want others to be awake, too.

My biggest concern, and not just for myself, has always been that we are not living life on purpose. It is just so easy to go through the motions, set ourselves on autopilot in no particular direction, do what we are expected to do because everyone else is doing it.

A friend of mine had a grandfather who was a farmer, like his father had been, and his father before him, and so on. And being a farmer is an honorable and good profession.

However, his grandfather never seemed happy. His life consisted of long days filled with back-breaking work, and my friend recalls that there was always just something grim about him. And his grandfather was good at other things. He was articulate and loved to read; he was a born storyteller. His eyes would light up when he was telling about something he had read, or a story or joke he'd heard. My friend always wondered if his grandfather would have been happier as a teacher or a minister (he was also deeply religious).

I will always remember these words he said about him: "My grandfather was a farmer, but he never asked himself if this was what he wanted to do with his life. It never even occurred to him to ask."

There's a famous story about Thomas Huxley, a nineteenth-century English biologist, anthropologist, and advocate of evolution, who did quite a bit of lecturing and debating. He once dashed out of one speaking engagement on his way to another, getting into the horse-drawn carriage waiting for him, thinking his driver knew what the destination was.

As he got in, he yelled, "I'm late! Drive very fast!" So, the driver took off. But after a few minutes, it didn't seem to Huxley like they were going in the right direction, so he yelled up again, "Do you know where you're going?" And the driver yelled back, "I have no idea where I am going. But I am driving very fast!"

Our lives can be like that. I'm not sure that most of us know where we're going. We can dash around in every direction, without ever questioning where or why.

I heard one person claim that unhappiness is not knowing what we want and then killing ourselves to get it. Someone else has said we often find ourselves, "Buying things we don't want, with money we don't have, to impress people we don't like."

The great Southern preacher Fred Craddock would sometimes make up far-fetched scenarios in his sermons to make his point. He once described a big old spotted greyhound he met in someone's home he was visiting. The greyhound had once been a racer that would chase a mechanical rabbit around a track, and Craddock started talking to the dog.

He asked, "So, are you still racing any?"

And the dog said, "No, no, I don't race anymore."

"Well, do you miss the excitement and glitter of the track?" he asked.

"No. Not really," said the dog.

"Well, what's the matter? Did you get too old?"

"No, no, I still had some race left in me."

"Well, did you not win?"

"No, I won over a million dollars for my owner. I was still winning."

"Then what was it? Did they treat you bad?"

"Oh no, they treated us royally when we were racing."

"Did you get hurt or injured?"

"No, no, I was fine physically."

Craddock kept up his inquiries, "Then what? What happened?"

And the dog said, "I quit."

"You quit?"

"Yeah, that's what I said. I quit."

"Well, why'd you quit?"

And the dog said, "One day I discovered that what I was chasing was not really a rabbit. So, I quit." The dog looked Craddock right in the eye and said, "All that running and running and running, and chasing around that track, and what I was chasing wasn't even real!"

I think this silly illustration asks us something pretty deep of ourselves. It asks us to pause every once in a while and ask: What am I doing? What am I spending my time on? What am I using my talent and energy to pursue? What am I giving my life to, day after day? Is it worthwhile? Does it have meaning? Is it valuable and real in any ultimate sense? Eventually I will have spent all the time

I have been given, I will have used up my whole life. I don't want it all to be gone only to discover when it's too late that what I was chasing wasn't even real.

Blaise Pascal, the seventeenth-century French philosopher, once wrote, "All of humanity's problems stem from man's inability to sit quietly in a room alone." Now, he didn't mean for us to sit in a room all the time, just often enough to press the pause button on the intense trajectory our lives can take. Just long enough to ask yourself some of these deep questions of life, the deepest of which, I think, is simply: What am I doing with my life? Does it have any meaning? Is it what I desire to be doing at a deep-seated level of my soul? Because one day my life will be over; this is the one and only life that I have been given, and it will have consisted of the value and meaning I have put into it day after day.

Am I chasing money the whole time, position, trying to get to the top of some corporate ladder or organizational pyramid? Is it fame that I'm after, recognition? Do I want power, the ability to force others to see things my way and do what I want? We may not want to think too hard about what we are doing because just asking the right questions may reveal how shallow our pursuits truly are. Are these things that I am giving my life to authentic and genuine?

I have found that so many personal transformations begin with the simple question: Is this all there is?

My experience is that most of us automatically assume that because we are busy our lives have meaning, when I wonder if it is not just the opposite. But when we give ourselves a place and a time to be alone with only our thoughts to keep us company, we may begin to ponder how we can spend our time doing what has some eternal value and purpose: building character and inner substance in our lives, creating a better and more hopeful world, investing in the lives of other people.

So, what if we wake up at 60? Actually, I think we can wake up at any age, whether it's even quite a bit older or much younger.

What if you wake up to the fact that you never became the person you were born to be? What if you begin to ask: Was there something I was supposed to be doing with my life?

Anthony Burgess was diagnosed with an inoperable brain tumor at the age of 40 and told that he had a year to live. He had to quit his job and didn't have any money to leave his family for their support after he was gone.

He decided to take the one year he had left and write a novel. He'd always wanted to write and thought he could come up with something pretty good, making as much money at that as anything else. So, he began to write, and he got completely engrossed in it; he loved it, loved every minute of writing it. At the end of the year, he finished his novel, and it was published and did pretty well.

What was more, at the end of that one year, he wasn't dead. So, he decided to write a second novel, and a third after that, and a fourth, and a fifth. In the middle of his sixth novel, he thought to himself, "You know, I might not be dying right now."

In fact, it had been a misdiagnosis; he did not have a brain tumor. During the remainder of his 36 more years of life, he wrote a total of 73 novels, the most recognized of which is *A Clockwork Orange*. It was named by *Time* magazine and *Modern Library* as one of the 100 best English-language novels of the twentieth century and later turned into a highly acclaimed movie. Anthony Burgess was completely absorbed with life once he got started.

What if you lived like that? What if you lived completely? What if you decided you weren't going to do what everyone else was doing, or what everyone expected you to do? What if you decided to go your own way? What if you became the person you were born to be?

I love this quote by Henry David Thoreau: "You must live in the present, launch yourself on every wave, find your eternity in each moment."

Do you know the song, "Live Like You Were Dying"? It's a country song performed by Tim McGraw and it's about a man in his early forties who learns that his father has an unspecified, life-threatening illness. After looking at the X-rays and talking about the options, it was realized that this might really be the end.

So, the son asked his father what did you do when you got that kind of news? And his father's answer is (feel free to sing along here if you know it): "I went skydiving. I went Rocky Mountain climbing. I went 2.7 seconds on a bull named Fu Manchu. And I loved deeper. And I spoke sweeter. And I gave forgiveness I'd been denying."

I love those words, although the payoff for me isn't in his doing all of the bucket list adventure kinds of stuff—especially because no matter how short of a time I might have to live, if it were me, I would never skydive or ride a bull with any name for any length of time. No, for me, the deeper part of the change that occurs in the father is his living as a person of character and loving and forgiving others in a way that is infectious in the time he has left.

In fact, the best part of the song is when the son, who isn't facing a terminal illness himself, makes the decision that living spectacularly in the moment is simply the best way to live. He finally became "the husband that most of the time I wasn't, and . . . a friend a friend would like to have." He goes on to say, "I finally read the Good Book, and took a good, long, hard look [his Blaise

Pascal sitting-in-a-room-alone moment] at what I'd do if I could do it all again." And then he decides, like his father, to skydive, to climb and ride the bull, as well as to love deeper and speak sweeter and give forgiveness.

Now, I know, it's kind of a sappy song, but it really does describe for me the way we are supposed to live, with its emphasis on love and forgiveness and relationship and character. The only thing I disagree with is the suggestion that you really only wake up to what's important when time is running out. I don't think you have to have a heart attack or a brain tumor diagnosis in order to be motivated to begin to ask the deep questions of life or live the right way.

I think all you need is to just wake up a little bit to the possibilities of your life and then make the decision to pursue them.

I heard about this woman who was dying of cancer, and her husband got up the courage to ask her, "What's it feel like knowing that you're dying?" And her answer was, "What does it feel like pretending that you're not?" Live full today and leave it all on the field, in other words, whether you have many more todays or this is your last one.

The truth is that we're all dying, and to live as if today is all we have just simply makes the most sense, not just because today may end up to be all you have, but because we really should want all of our todays added together to be the most productive, loving, and fun we can make them.

I like what a young man by the name of Kyle Idleman, a minister in Louisville, Kentucky, says: "Listen to me, I don't know what it's going to take, but I know you don't have to hit rock bottom. You can wake up now. You can come to your senses today."

One of the ways we can come to our senses today is expressed in Daniel Pink's great book, *Drive*. He recounts a conversation between Clare Boothe Luce, one of the first women to serve in the U. S. Congress, and President John F. Kennedy. "A great man," she told him, "is one sentence." She described Abraham Lincoln's sentence as: "He preserved the Union and freed the slaves." Franklin Roosevelt's sentence, she told him, was: "He lifted us out of a great depression and helped us win a world war."

Congresswoman Luce was afraid at the time that Kennedy's attention was so splintered among different priorities that his sentence risked becoming a muddled paragraph. We could talk now about what Kennedy's own sentence might be: "He challenged us to land a man on the moon," or "He stood up to the Soviet Union but kept the peace."

The question is: What is *your* sentence? What is the one sentence you would like people to say about you? Like Kennedy, we run the risk that our priorities will be splintered and our lives become muddled and confused. One way to wake up to what your life might be is to think of the sentence you would like to readily come to people's minds when they think about you.

Maybe your sentence is about your vocation: "He wrote a book that gave people hope." "She was a doctor who saved lives." "He was a fair and honest lawyer." "She loved teaching and it showed every day with every child." "He was a custodian, and this place was spotless." "She volunteered in the community and helped countless people."

Or perhaps your sentence would be more about your personal attributes or your character: "She had a kind word and smile for everyone." "He never held a grudge; he was quick to forgive and move on." "When you think of the word 'joy,' you think of her." "You could go to him with any problem and he would always try to help."

My co-author and his wife love to travel to Great Britain and have been there many times. On one trip, they trekked out into the English countryside to see an ornate little church they had heard about. Over the entrance are these words: "In the year 1653, when all things through the land were either demolished or profaned, Sir Robert Shirley, Baronet, built this church, whose singular praise was to do the best things in the worst of times and to have hoped them in the most difficult."

The Chapel of the Holy Trinity at Staunton Harold, built by Sir Robert Shirley.

This was during the English Civil War, when things did indeed seem to be falling apart. But you don't need a history lesson to appreciate that here was a principled man who was true and hopeful even when it was not easy. What if your sentence was, "He did his best when things were at their worst," or "She gave hope in the most difficult of times?"

William Gladstone and Benjamin Disraeli dominated politics and were the leaders of their respective parties in Great Britain for much of the nineteenth century. They each served several times as prime minister. There is the story of one woman who sat next to each of them on separate occasions at state dinners, and she summed up her impressions of each in one sentence: "When you were with Gladstone, you felt like you were *with* the most important person in the world. When you were with Disraeli, you felt like *you* were the most important person in the world."

What's your sentence, that you make people think you're the most important person in the world, or do you make them feel like they are the most important? Which do you want it to be?

It might be helpful to first try to think about what your sentence is right now. This can be sobering. Can you be candid enough with yourself to figure out how others might describe you today in one sentence?

Of course, it might be positive; you might already be living into the great person you desire to be. It might be negative, though; your sentence right now might leave a lot of room for improvement: "He settled for that job when he could've been so much more." "She got to the top of that company but walked over everybody to get there." "He had everything money could buy, but nothing money couldn't buy." "She was always bitter after it happened." "He never had time for anybody." "She simply would not compromise on anything." "He was always talking." "She had a pretty mean temper."

Alfred Nobel was a Swedish chemist, engineer, and inventor in the nineteenth century. He held many patents, but he is best known for his invention of dynamite. He amassed a fortune through his company's manufacture of explosives and armaments.

Nobel was living in France when his brother died. A local newspaper in Paris mistakenly thought it was Alfred who had passed away and printed his obituary. It said, "the merchant of death is dead," going on to say that he "became rich by finding ways to kill more people faster than ever before."

Alfred Nobel.

Nobel was appalled and heartbroken. He had never thought of what he did in those terms and did not want to be remembered that way. He did not want that to be his sentence.

He decided that he was going to leave a legacy of a whole different kind. So, he left a few small bequests to his extended family (he had no wife or children) and to friends and servants. But the vast bulk of his estate was put in trust, "the interest on which shall be annually distributed in the form of prizes to those who, in the preceding year, shall have conferred the greatest benefit to mankind."

This is how the Nobel prizes began. There are five categories: Physics, Chemistry, Medicine, Literature, and, of course, Peace. He did not want to be remembered for dynamite and armaments. He wanted to be known—and he is most well-known—for the Nobel Peace Prize. Alfred Nobel had the supreme gift of reading his obituary while he could still change the course of his life.

I don't know of a faster way to be motivated to re-direct yourself toward a more positive, healthy, and productive life destination than to write what you would like the sentence of your life to be or envision your own obituary.

It might happen, of course, after a heart attack or a diagnosis of cancer, a nearly fatal traffic accident, a close call of some sort that compels you to review your life. I described that happening to me in the last chapter. The thing is, though, that most people do not change in the long run after such an incident.

They may change for a while; they may say they're going to change. But most do not change their behavior; they go back to the way they were before. Studies suggest this, and so does our own observation of human behavior.

Dr. Edward Miller, former CEO of the hospital at Johns Hopkins University and former dean of the medical school there, did some research on this. He studied patients with heart disease that was so severe they had to undergo bypass surgery, a traumatic and expensive procedure. But once successful, these surgeries provide a real chance for change for the patients. Because of the surgeries, they can now, through lifestyle changes, stave off pain and even death if they're willing to act on the opportunity. But according to Dr. Miller's research, the change rarely takes place.

He writes, "If you look at people after coronary-artery bypass surgery two years later, 90 percent of them have not changed their lifestyle. And that's been studied over and over and over again . . . Even though they know they have a very bad disease and they know they should change their lifestyle—they know, in a very real sense, that they must change or die—for whatever reason, they can't."

Most people don't start eating better after a health scare. They don't start exercising. They don't slow down when they're told that stress is killing them. They don't become kinder when people intervene and tell them they are rude and obnoxious. They don't become more grateful for life when it's almost taken away. They don't appreciate each day more just because they have suddenly become startlingly aware of the fact that life is finite.

Most people simply do not change to a more physically or emotionally healthy way of life.

Some do, many do. And most importantly, *you can*. You just have to be willing to wake up to what you want to be.

The invitation is always there to change, to re-write your story, to seek a different destination. You have to be willing, though, to do something like come up with the sentence you want for your life or write the obituary you desire to live into. You have to want to wake up. You have to want to be the thermostat and not a thermometer.

And it is then that the real work begins. It is then that you have to decide to do something to make that sentence or obituary come true. You can't just intend to do it at some vague future time; you have to decide that this is the way you want to live.

So much of life is what you decide it will be. We are what we repeatedly decide to do. A good life takes time; it is the accumulation of all of the decisions we make.

I heard about a road sign in Canada for what was actually a dirt road that was muddy in the summer and frozen into crusty grooves or tracks in the winter. The sign said, "Driver, choose carefully which rut you drive in, you'll be in it for the next 20 miles."

The same is true of our lives. The decisions we make place us into a track or groove or rut. They can help speed us on our way toward our envisioned destination or take us just as quickly the wrong way. We have to be careful where our decisions place us, because we can only with great difficulty break out of the rut (whether good or bad) that we get ourselves into.

Similarly, Horace Mann, the educator, once said, "Habit is like a cable; we weave a strand of it every day, and in the end it cannot be broken." Our decisions are reinforced and strengthened by every subsequent decision we make in the same direction. Habits are hard to break. Bad habits can be broken, though, if you begin to make different decisions that loosen their hold on you and start a reversal of the process.

It may not seem like it, but we are making decisions all the time that are sending us in certain directions. I still remember and believe very strongly in what someone told me some years ago: "You are the same today as you'll be in five years except for two things: the books you read and the people you meet."

Not everything we read is good for us. Not all that we see in books or articles or the screen time on our computer or smartphone is inspiring, healthy, and productive for us. We have to be careful with what we fill our minds. Each decision what to read is taking us somewhere.

In the same way, not every person we encounter—not every friend, not everyone in our family—is good for us. Some people can bring you down, be discouraging, make you feel hopeless.

There's an old story of a man who was standing on the ledge of a tall building because he was going to jump. A policeman crawled out to try and talk him down, but the man steadfastly refused to be talked out of it. Finally, the man agreed to listen to the policeman list all of the things that were good about the world, if the man could in turn give his list of all that was awful with the world.

The policeman first mentioned everything he could think of that was good, and then the man gave his long list of all that was terrible. And when he was finished, the man and the policeman both decided to jump.

We have to be careful of the people and ideas we allow to have access to our minds and hearts. We need to seek out those who are uplifting and encouraging and hopeful. I know it's not always up to us who we associate with in family or work or community settings, but we need to try as much as we can to search for those positive relationships.

The only exception is if we are with a negative person because we want to help that person become healthier in some way. We don't let them bring us down; we try to build them up. "He gave hope to hopeless people," is a great sentence to have as a goal.

Listening is another decision we can make. Most of us think that we're either good listeners or we're not, that it's in our nature, and likewise that we are natural-born talkers or not. I'll leave the discussion of one's ability to talk to people or speak in public for another time, but I do believe that we can decide and learn to listen. We may have to decide intellectually that it is good for us, there is value, if we listen.

It is probably a decision we need to make ahead of time, as we go into a meeting, let's say, that this time I will not speak, I will listen. In the moment, we may need to decide to literally bite our tongue to keep from talking, and listen. And gradually, the decisions will add up and reinforce themselves and become second nature, and we will become better at listening. It was Aristotle who said, "Wisdom is the reward for a lifetime of listening when you would rather be talking."

You can probably see where this is headed, that I am suggesting to you that just about everything in life is a decision. I would even suggest that it is possible for you to make the decision to be happy.

This is a pretty bold claim, but whether or not you are happy is the result of the decisions you make in your life. Now, probably most people would say that happiness is a feeling or an emotion, the result of what happens to you; you have no real control over it. Sometimes you feel happy, they would say, depending on the circumstances, and sometimes you feel unhappy. But your sentence can be, "She was a happy person and shared her happiness with others," and you can make decisions that will make it be so.

Your first decision might be to do some research on what happiness is, read some books on it, see what some of the great minds say who have thought deeply about it. You might think deeply yourself about such concepts as "pleasure" and "gratification" and "enjoyment" and "contentment" and "satisfaction" and "blessedness." All are definitions and synonyms for happiness, and there are many more, but they don't all mean the same thing or lead in the same direction.

You may discover that happiness is found, counterintuitively, it would seem, in serving others. I have thought long and hard about Albert Schweitzer's claim in his commencement address at a boys' school: "I do not know what your destiny will be, but one thing I know: the only ones among you who will be truly happy are those who will have sought and found how to serve." I have always found his words to be true, but you have to live with them for a while, try them on for size in your own life.

One of the simplest things to do to start down the path of the happiness decision is to ask yourself periodically, "What would a happy person do right now, in the circumstances in which I find myself?" and then make the decision to do that. It may be the hardest to do of all of your alternatives, the most inconvenient, the most time-consuming, but if it is the decision that will begin to reinforce and strengthen the bond of happiness in your life, it is what you must do.

Or you might need to ask yourself, "What decisions am I making that are contributing to my *un*happiness?" and stop making those kinds of decisions.

Norman Vincent Peale wrote about a woman he knew who ran into an old friend and they got to talking. The other woman asked what her husband did for a living, and she thought for a moment before answering, "He's in the manufacturing business." And the other woman said, "Oh really, the manufacturing business. What does he manufacture?" And the first woman said, "Unhappiness. He manufactures his own unhappiness." It no doubt took this man years of these kinds of decisions, a whole lifetime of destructive decisions, to reach this point where his wife was willing to share the end result with her friend.

I want to tell you that, if this is you, you can stop doing this. But you have to decide that it is what you want to do. You may have to turn things in a different direction with the decisions you now are making, loosen that cable of habit that has been strangling you, and reinforce the decisions that will lead to your habit of happiness.

I'm not saying it will be easy. Happiness is one of the more challenging areas to discuss and decisions to make. These are just some suggestions to get you started.

I simply want to plant this seed in you, that happiness is a decision. It is *your* decision.

So are things like hope and joy and patience and peace. The list really does go on and on. You might ask yourself, "What would a hopeful person do in my circumstances?" as you think about the decisions you are soon going to be making. And you don't have to be having a difficult time in your life to think about hope. If your goal is to live with hope, if your sentence has anything to do with being hopeful or bringing hope to people, ask yourself periodically, "Am I living as a hopeful person? Am I making decisions that are hopeful?"

"What would a joyful person do?" is another question we might ask ourselves from time to time. A patient person? What would a person who longs to be at peace with others and with the world and with him- or herself do today, or this week, or in the midst of this (whatever the stress may be)?

The decisions you make each day leading toward or away from the destination you have set for yourself, will largely determine what your life will turn out to be.

Norman Cousins was editor-in-chief of the *Saturday Review* and at the age of 49 was diagnosed with ankylosing spondylitis (which causes inflammation and fusion of vertebrae and joints) and connective tissue disease (a degenerative disease causing the breakdown of collagen, or connective tissue, in the body). It left him in almost constant pain and the doctor told him he had one chance in 500 for any kind of recovery and gave him only six months to live.

This diagnosis came right after a stressful trip, and Cousins could see how worry, depression, and anger contributed to, and perhaps helped cause, his disease. He wondered to himself, "If illness can be caused by things that are negative, can wellness be created by things that are positive?"

He decided to make a kind of experiment of himself. He exercised, took massive amounts of vitamin C, and ate healthy. He spent as much time as he could with family and friends. But the most important part of his regimen was laughter. Laughter was one of the most positive activities he knew. He rented all the funny movies he could. This was before Netflix and DVDs and videos, so he had to rent the actual films. He read funny stories. He asked his friends to call him whenever they heard about or did something funny.

And gradually, his condition began to improve. His pain had been so great at first that he could not sleep. But he discovered that ten minutes of genuine belly laughter had an anesthetic effect and would give him at least two hours of pain-free sleep when nothing else, not even morphine, would help. Slowly he regained the use of his limbs.

Within six months he was back on his feet, and in two years he had returned to his work full-time. He later wrote a book about his disease and recovery with the title, *Anatomy of an Illness from the Perspective of the Patient*. In all, he lived 26 years after his bleak diagnosis. He lived years that were engaged and healthy and full of laughter, because he made the decision that this would be his life.

Step Five

What is your sentence? What is it now? What would you like it to be? What do you want your obituary to say? What one or two or three things might you decide to do right now to get your life to move in that direction? Pause and think about what it means to live in the present, to live like you were dying? What would you decide to do if you knew that today was the last day of your life? Is there any reason not to start doing those things?

POSSESSING OR BEING POSSESSED

Believe In God

High-school seniors Heather Brown and Tyler Smith were at a beach near St. Augustine, Florida, with a group of friends to celebrate the annual senior skip day. The two went for a swim in the choppy water. They were both strong swimmers, but without realizing it, they began to be carried out to sea by the current. They tried to swim back, but instead of coming closer to shore, they could see they were actually getting farther away.

"That's when we started to freak out," Tyler recalled later. They were desperate, exhausted, and two miles from land. Heather asked him, "Tyler, my God, we're stuck. What's the plan?" They knew that if they kept swimming, they would soon tire and drown. So, the plan became simply to link arms and float together—and pray: "God, if you're out there, please send something to save us."

About 30 minutes later, a boat traveling from South Florida to New Jersey spotted them. "It came out of nowhere," Heather said. Her immediate thought was, "God is real! When I saw the boat, I knew we were getting out of here."

When they were safely aboard and given blankets to warm up, the captain had one more surprise for the two teenagers—the name of the boat was *Amen*. It was as if the boat came in direct answer to their prayer. The captain later said he felt "God had sent him there" because the boat wasn't really supposed to be there at the time. They were already scheduled to depart for the north, but the rough water made the crew of the *Amen* decide to wait it out, which meant they were there for the rescue.

I love these kinds of stories, ones that can't be explained merely by chance and happenstance. There's an element of something beyond us at work here, something we can't quite account for or fully understand, a higher power creating something good when it could have been a disaster, a plan where there seemed to be nothing but vast, empty ocean and manifest oblivion.

This was certainly Heather's feeling after her rescue. She said bluntly, "God obviously has a plan for us."

In 2017, there were terrible tornadoes, along with rain and flooding, in East Texas. We hear of these kinds of things there and in other parts of the country every year, but this was a particularly brutal season. A young family was watching the news and heard of a tornado headed right for them, so they bundled their two children into their pickup truck and tried to make a run for it. But they ran into furious winds and the truck hydroplaned, placing it upside down in a nearby ditch filled with several feet of rainwater.

Other people on the road saw this happen and came swiftly to the rescue. (This part was caught on a smartphone camera and has been uploaded onto YouTube.) They plunged into water above their waists and struggled with the doors of the truck. When they broke through the windows and got the doors open, they saw the mother and father, struggling to get free, but basically okay. But then they saw the children—a two-year-old girl and an infant boy—still trapped in the water. Neither of them was breathing, and you could hear the rescuers' voices growing frantic in the video. They pulled the children out of the water and put them in the back of another vehicle and started doing CPR.

Most of the time, you could hear a woman talking in the background, trying to provide encouragement and moral support to the rescuers. But when she learned the children weren't breathing, she began to pray, "Dear Jesus, please let this baby breathe! In the name of Jesus, let this baby breathe!" She didn't stop, she kept praying.

The man doing CPR on one of the children later said, "At the first prayer, I felt a response in that child." First one and then the other began to breathe. One of the children had to spend a little time in the hospital, but the other was declared to be fit at the scene and the prognosis was that both would make a full and complete recovery.

These stories, I have to tell you, send a bit of shiver through me. What if there is an unseen power at work in the world? Sometimes it's hard to tell that it's there, frankly; plenty of bad things do happen, teenagers do drown in the ocean, babies do die in accidents. But sometimes this power is unmistakable and unstoppable!

What if there is power, and what if it's not just out there somewhere but is close at hand, at work in your life? Or, what if it could be if you recognized it and received it? What if you were open to another dimension of life? What if you operated your life as if there were something more—or someone—ready to be called upon and ready to call you to something higher and greater? What if you said yes and lived with an expectation, an anticipation, an eagerness to be inspired and challenged to something beyond anything you have ever known?

This book is about how people who might be living below their potential can take ownership of their lives, be bolder in what they see and attempt, and believe in the capacity of their thoughts and actions to bring transformation. We have such untapped promise and potential in us.

But I would suggest there is a higher power too, and this higher power, or God, may be for you and me the untapped resource beyond any other. I believe we can be inspired and challenged in ways that are absolute and enduring. We can take ownership of having a relationship with this higher power. We can be bold in what we ask, seek, and hope. And we can believe in God's capacity to rescue, save, and change us and the world.

What if there is a presence and a power—and it's closer than you think? I remember an old story of a father and son who were out walking and came across a sizeable stone along the way. The boy asked his father, "Dad, do you think I'm strong enough to move this stone?" The father thought it over for a moment and responded, "Yes, son, you're strong enough to move the stone, as long as you use every resource you have." So, the boy tried to move the stone. His first attempt was to pick it up, but it was too big and there was no way he could do that. Then, he tried to push the stone over onto its side, but the stone simply wouldn't budge. After a couple of attempts, the boy gave up and said, "Well Dad, I guess you were wrong. I'm not strong enough to move that stone."

But the father said, "Son, you are strong enough. But I said you would have to use every resource you had. You didn't use every resource. You didn't use me to help you." With that, the son eagerly went back to work, this time with the assistance of his father, and together they easily pushed it over onto its side.

As you attempt to take ownership of your life, are you using every resource at your disposal? I love the words of Scottish runner and Olympic champion Eric Liddell, who was also an ordained pastor and missionary. His story was immortalized in the movie *Chariots of Fire*. Talking about how he was able to win a particular race, Liddell said, "In the first half, I ran as fast as I could. In the second half, with God's help, I ran faster." We may have skill and be bold and do fairly well on our own, but how much faster and better might we run in the race of life with God's assistance and direction?

A plaque at the University of Edinburgh honoring Eric Liddell.

I heard about a man by the name of Paul who experienced something really quite amazing when he was a soldier during the Korean War. He was out on a scouting patrol and somehow got lost and wandered into enemy territory. For several days he hid out in the wilderness, but eventually he was captured and made a prisoner of war. It was a horrific experience beyond words.

In addition to the despicable physical conditions for the prisoners, his captors engaged in psychological torment. On two occasions, for example, Paul was compelled by the enemy to dig his own grave and then stand in front of it as a firing squad marched out, raised their rifles, took aim, and squeezed their triggers.

Nothing happened though—the rifles did not fire, the hammers fell shut on empty chambers. It was a form of torture that took its toll on Paul's mind.

On another occasion, in the midst of the cold North Korean winter, his captors poured ice water on Paul's head over and over again, bucket after bucket, until he became the victim of complete amnesia. I don't know if that's what they intended to do, but it was the result. He could not remember anything: who he was, where he was, where he came from, or what he was doing there. He didn't even know his name. Day after day, night after night, hour after hour, he sat in that prison camp, trying desperately to remember something, anything, out of his suddenly darkened past. It seemed like the only thing he could remember was that he couldn't remember.

Finally, after a long struggle, he remembered two words: "Our Father."

Just those two words. He didn't know what they meant or where they came from, but he knew they represented something important from his past. So, he began to repeat those two words—"Our Father . . . Our Father . . . Our Father"—hoping something else would come back to him out of his lost memory.

Well, something did come: "Our Father, who art in heaven." Then he repeated that phrase over and over until he remembered, "hallowed be thy name." He went on like that until he reconstructed the entire Lord's Prayer. Then he began to remember other things: his parents who had taught him this prayer and the church where he recited it with other worshippers every Sunday morning. Then he remembered his neighborhood, his friends, his country, his mission there in Korea as a soldier. And finally, he remembered his name!

His whole memory and life were rebuilt around those two words, "Our Father." It was as if he turned his life over to those two words and this prayer and ultimately to the higher power embodied in it. Interestingly and ironically, he got something out of this experience he never had before: a photographic memory. Turning over our lives like this to a power beyond us is what I am suggesting

George Frideric Handel.

here as a way to discover ourselves, to build and, when necessary, rebuild our lives, and to be given what we need for the present and future.

Ray Johnston, in a great book called *The Hope Quotient*, put it this way: "Whatever you need, God is greater. Whatever you're going through, God is bigger. Whatever your weakness, God is stronger. Raise your expectation of what God can do. Raise your expectation of what God will do with you."

One of the greatest musical compositions in history is the work of George Frideric Handel, which is simply called *Messiah*. A friend presented Handel with a new libretto one day, based on the life of Christ, the entire script of which was from the Bible. According to stories about the famed masterpiece, Handel was so enthusiastic about it that he immediately shut himself up in his home in London and, absorbed in this composition and hardly eating or drinking, he completed the work, including all of the arrangements for chorus and orchestration, in 24 breathtaking days.

Later, as he groped for words to describe what he had experienced, he said, "Whether I was in the body or out of my body when I wrote it, I do not know." At one point during its composition, his servant walked into the room to plead with him to eat, and he saw Handel with tears streaming down his face, saying, "I did think I did see all Heaven before me, and the great God Himself!"

Handel was in the grasp of something beyond himself that took him to a whole different realm of creativity and inspiration. It's almost like he was possessed. The writer Willa Cather defined happiness this way: "to be dissolved into something complete and great." It was the theologian Paul Tillich who said being grasped by a power greater than we are is the very essence of faith and belief.

We have been talking about the power of faith and belief throughout this book. Believing in your inner voice, for example, and believing in the capacity to visualize your future, believing in the power of your purpose. Certainly, the concept of belief is indispensable when we talk about God and religious thought. The thing is that when most people talk about belief as a religious idea, it is usually belief about an objective statement or set of facts that they think, or believe, is true. We say, "I believe in the Articles of Religion," for example, or, "I believe in the Apostles' Creed." In other words, I believe these facts and statements about God, or about Jesus Christ.

But the origins of the word "believe" had a person as its direct object, not a statement. It did not originally mean to believe a declaration or affirmation or creed was true and factual; it was more like what we mean today when we say to someone, "I believe in you." Belief comes from an old English word meaning "to hold dear," which connotes confidence in, intimacy with, and even love for a person. To believe and to belove are considered synonyms.

It's not belief in a set of principles, it's belief in a person, God. It's not that we know facts about God but that we know *him*, or at least we are trying to know him and develop that relationship. There is a sense of belonging and assurance and trust. Or, as I heard one person say, "To believe means to lean your whole weight on God."

Dietrich Bonhoeffer was a German theologian and pastor whose prime years were lived in Nazi Germany. He publicly opposed Hitler, for which he spent the last two years of his life in prison. He lost everything, including his own life at the age of 39, when he was hanged at Flossenbürg concentration camp a month before the end of World War II.

He lost everything, and yet he left his prison cell for his execution saying, "This is the end, but for me the beginning of life." Like Handel, he was grasped and possessed by a power greater than his own.

Bonhoeffer expressed this beautifully in a poem he wrote just days before his execution, where he asks the question, "Who am I?" He goes through a number of possibilities, listing some good qualities about himself that others admire, like being calm and composed in the face of death. But he also lists other things only he knows about himself that are not nearly so appealing: that he is "restless and longing and sick, . . . weary and empty at praying."

He sees that he is full of irony and contradiction, as we all are, and he makes no final conclusion as to who he is except to say, "Whoever I am, Thou knowest, O God, I am Thine."

This is the essence of belief. With this higher power, there is relationship, intimacy, belonging, assurance, confidence, trust. In this sense, taking ownership of my life here means to let go of my life, to make the decision to place myself into the hands of the one I know I can trust. There is a sense of release, of losing control, of turning my life over, of surrendering it completely, of being grasped and possessed by one on whom I can rely no matter what may happen to me, even to the point of death and beyond.

I have a friend who used to play golf. She was pretty good at one point and spent quite a bit of time practicing her game. But she had a peculiar ritual as she addressed the ball and teed off. She would get in her stance, ready to swing just the way she had practiced and visualized over and over, but just before she would take her swing, she would say to herself, "I don't care." Any of you who are real golfers will be laughing at this, but she thought it helped her game and gave her an edge. She thought it relaxed her to the point that all of her skills could come alive in a more natural, less forced, way. Sometimes when you care too much and try to control everything, it places too much pressure on you and interferes physically and mentally with what you could do if you just let go a little bit. My friend was able to relax but, at the same time, swing more powerfully because she knew that it didn't all depend on her, that a certain percentage of the game was beyond her.

In every endeavor, we know there is a limit to how far our abilities will take us. Sometimes the same skill and attitude and daring will take you to the Super Bowl, and sometimes they will not even get you into the playoffs. In 2019 Tiger Woods won the Masters one week and didn't even make the cut for the PGA Championship a month later. There are forces beyond our control, so it helps to mentally release the responsibility for the outcome and simply do the best we can.

Similarly, there is much in our lives that we can't control, no matter how much we take ownership of our problems and habits and attitudes, no matter how many decisions we make to better our lives. We simply don't have control over every outcome. We can worry and be frustrated and try to control what we know is beyond our control, or we can turn over some of that control to a higher power and place more and more of our trust in God. This is what I mean by being grasped and possessed by God, to surrender our control to one in whom we have confidence and assurance that he is working for our good, to know and believe in that one beyond any question. This is the essence of a life lived with faith and belief, to trust ever more deeply in God.

There was a large church I know of that was facing some difficulty. They had overextended themselves financially to build a large addition. As in any organization, especially large ones, it seemed everyone had his/her own agenda for the future and there was more infighting than usual about which way the church should go. What's more, a beloved senior pastor, one who had been able to hold it all together for many years, was getting ready to retire. The people in the pews were justifiably nervous about the future.

The church didn't always have an annual saying or motto to focus them for the year ahead, but occasionally they would develop one. That year, they decided to have one. The leadership team and pastor, after much prayer, settled on this motto for what they knew would be a year of intense pressure and transition: "Trust God No Matter What."

And "Trust God No Matter What" was more than just a motto; it became a way of life for that church. They took ownership over the decisions within their control: they made some difficult but prudent financial resolutions and they pulled out all the stops to find a new senior pastor who was intelligent and gracious and humble, who would inspire and challenge the congregation. But the greatest decision they made was to turn over responsibility for the outcome to God, to believe God had the very best in mind for the church.

A deep spirit of trusting God no matter what happened that year seemed to pervade and infuse the people. The entire atmosphere of the church seemed to be more positive and unified. Speaking that message of belief and hope into the church week after week did wonders.

I think in this way we can be even bolder in our lives by not being in control of everything. We do need to be bold in speaking positive and productive words to ourselves. We need to be bold in visualizing our future. We need to be bold in seizing the day and taking action. We need to be bold in overcoming difficulties and obstacles. We need to be bold in finding our purpose. But I would tell you that the boldest action we can take is the boldness of placing our lives and our futures into the possession of God. It's a boldness not in what we can do, but in what God can do. We must be bold in placing more of our lives into our own hands, but bolder still in placing more of our lives into the hands of God.

What I am encouraging you to do was stated as a powerful theological concept many years ago by Saint Augustine, when he famously said, "Work as if it all depends on you, and pray as if it all depends on God." When we are bold and disciplined with our thoughts and actions, positive things begin to happen. I

President Theodore Roosevelt.

hope you have discovered this already as you have put elements from the first five chapters into practice. But just as important is to be bold and disciplined in trusting God and turning more of your life over to this higher power, because good and positive things begin to happen then, too. As numerous people have told me over the years in one way or another, "It just seems like when I pray, God works. When I pray, coincidences begin to happen."

This is why we must be bold in approaching God, bold in seeking that relationship, bold in coming to an intense place of trust and confidence, bold in asking to be changed and transformed and renewed, bold in believing that God wants what is best for you.

President Theodore Roosevelt would always claim that what made him supremely bold in all the many things he attempted and accomplished was the memory of his father holding him securely in his arms when Theodore was a sick and fragile little boy. Asthma was his main problem, and sometimes in the middle of the night he could not catch his breath. His father would come into his room and carry him around in his arms for an hour or more at a time, sometimes even harnessing the horses and driving through the streets of New York City hoping that as the boy gulped in air, his breathing would clear and he would survive. Teddy would later write, "My father got me breath, he got me lungs, strength, life. I could breathe, I could sleep when he had me in his arms."

Like Roosevelt in the arms of his father, we can rest secure in the arms of our heavenly father (or perhaps the image that works best for you, which is also biblical, is of a heavenly mother). And once secure in a presence and power that we can trust and that is at work in us, we can attempt and dare and risk things with our lives. As I heard one person express it, "What can anyone do to me when the living God of the universe is with me?"

There is an old poem by Myra Brooks Welch titled "The Touch of the Master's Hand." It starts off at an auction; various items are being auctioned off, including an old violin that's all battered and scarred. There's hardly anything bid for this old violin, and it's about to be sold for a measly three dollars until a gray-haired old man comes forward and picks it up. He dusts it off, tightens the loose strings, and plays "a melody pure and sweet, as sweet as an angel sings." Then he sits down and the bidding begins again, only this time it goes not for three dollars, but for three thousand dollars.

People cheer, but some are confused. "What changed its value?" they ask. And the response is that what changed its value is the touch of the master's hand. The master knows what to do; he knows how to play it.

The poem ends with these words: "And many a man with life out of tune, and battered and scarred with sin, is auctioned cheap to the thoughtless crowd, much like the old violin. But the Master comes and the foolish crowd never can quite understand the worth of a soul and the change that's wrought by the touch of the Master's hand."

I think one of the core decisions we have to make on the road to meaning and success is whether or not we believe in the possibility of experiencing God and in the power of communicating with God and placing our lives into his hands.

Some of you, I'm sure, are eating this chapter up and wanting to go deeper. You already have a deep relationship with God and a meaningful prayer life. You could school my co-author and me on the power of experiencing and communicating with God.

But I'm sure there are others for whom God and prayer are more or less an abstract idea, something to talk about in certain circles or assent to as a theoretical concept. Perhaps you say you believe in it but make no real commitment to it. Many of us go through the motions of prayer without really expecting anything to happen. Still others may not believe in God at all and may feel you're doing just fine.

If you fall into either of these last two categories, I appeal to you to think more about the contents of this chapter and put it into action. Like the other steps in this book, the real power and meaning of this will only come when there is something intentional, meticulous, and daily about taking one step after another toward your destination. Here, the destination is to cultivate a relationship with God and experience the power of prayer. So, even if you don't believe or you think talk about God is just so many words with little meaning, if you commit yourself to the behavior we are describing here—prayer, meditation, Bible reading, asking God to be real to you—my experience is that the power of God always comes. And it will come to you! Honestly, you will never know if I am right that God is good for you unless you take me up on my challenge, as I hope you are doing with the other steps in this book.

The eminent nineteenth-century psychologist William James is quoted as saying, "I don't sing because I am happy. I am happy because I sing." What he was saying is that he doesn't wait for a good feeling like happiness to come along and then engage in the cheerful behavior of singing. Rather, if I commit myself to positive and productive behavior like singing, even if I don't want to, the inevitable byproduct and end result will be a positive and productive feeling like happiness. In this way, as I have argued in chapter five, happiness really is a decision we make and then work toward.

The power comes when we are bold and proactive in deciding on our behavior.

It is true with every step in this book. Choose the behavior that will get you to your destination, and you will reach it, if not always, most of the time. And it is true here— pray, expect, and believe in God, and the experience and power of God will come.

The key thing to all of this is really pretty simple: to be open to how God might work in your life, to what God might do for you and through you, to be ready, to be available. It's paying attention and listening and surrender. It's simple, as I say, but not easy—everything in our lives and in the world around us tells us to be constantly on the go. We like to talk more than listen and take control more than surrender. And yet, things begin to happen when we make ourselves available to God.

I have some friends who were living in Boston as a young married couple with a small child. He was from there, but she was from Pittsburgh and wanted to return. They both did, actually, but had no idea how they might accomplish it. He had the kind of job he'd always wanted, in the industry and even with the company he loved. But his employer had almost no corporate presence in

Pittsburgh, so there was no chance for a lateral or even slightly downward move. They prayed about it and decided to simply be open to living and doing whatever God wanted of them. No one besides the two of them—and God—knew anything about Pittsburgh.

A few weeks later, one of his bosses came to him and said, "I know you probably don't have the slightest interest in this, but we are starting something new in Pittsburgh and you would be perfect for the job." He and his family not only moved to Pittsburgh, but he also got a promotion.

My friend was not one for expressing much drama outwardly, and he didn't as he told me the story. His only understated comment about the whole thing was, "It was as if there was a plan." Exactly! A plan, a design, a destination that God has in mind for us when we are open.

I know some people who say this prayer every day: "O God, let me be open to receive something unexpectedly good today. O God, let me be open to give something unexpectedly good to someone else today." Just saying these words to God and to yourself, especially on a daily basis over an extended period of time, will create an openness and expectancy in your life.

I have said that prayer at times but my prayer now, which is similar, is, "O God, I'm not looking for blessings to come into my life; I'm looking to be a blessing. Please make me a blessing today." I get on my knees and say this prayer every day, and something always happens. A few months back, a woman I had never met called and told me that her son had seen me on ESPN four years ago. She said he bought my book, *The Sender*, and it changed his life. He became a Christian and a much kinder person. She told me her son was gone now, but the last four years were the best of his life. We talked for a while; she was a wonderful person with a big heart and beautiful spirit. I don't know what the issues were that her son faced or what ultimately took his life at too young an age; she didn't say, and I didn't ask. But she wanted to tell me about her son and thank me. O God, I'm not looking for blessings to come into my life, I'm looking to be a blessing. Please make me a blessing.

We will talk more about this in our last chapter, but it's in seeking to be a blessing—and turning our lives over to God for him to make of us a blessing—that we go from being merely successful at what we do to living a life of great significance.

Repeating the Prayer of St. Francis can help us find this in ourselves:

> Lord, make me an instrument of your peace,
> Where there is hatred, let me sow peace,
> Where there is injury, pardon,

Where there is doubt, faith,
Where there is despair, hope,
Where there is darkness, light,
And where there is sadness, joy.
O Divine Master,
Grant that I may not seek so much
      to be consoled as to console,
To be understood as to understand,
To be loved as to love.
For it is in giving that we receive,
It is in pardoning that we are pardoned,
And it is in dying that we are born to eternal life.

Step Six

In what areas of your life have you begun to realize that you have little control? Make the decision to turn over control in that area to God. Say to yourself each morning five times, "I will trust God no matter what." Believe God wants what is best for you. Live with this as your attitude. Base every decision on this promise. In what ways do you need to be more open to God? Try saying the prayer, "O God, let me be open to receive something unexpectedly good today. O God, let me be open to give something unexpectedly good to someone today."

7

SHAKEN OR STIRRED

Believe In Your Past

On December 10, 2005, Sosoliso Airlines Flight 1145 took off from the airport in Abuja, Nigeria. The DC-9 was full and included 60 students from the local boarding school. They were traveling home for Christmas, and the mood must have been festive and buoyant. Two hours later, after an uneventful flight, the pilot announced that they would be landing soon at Nigeria's Port Harcourt International Airport.

But something went wrong. The weather was suddenly stormy, the visibility poor. The pilot waved off the first landing attempt and turned to make a new approach, but the altimeter was off or the pilot misread it, and instead the plane slammed into the ground and burst into flames.

Of 110 onboard—103 passengers and seven crewmembers—there were two survivors.

One, a 16-year-old girl, had third-degree burns over 65 percent of her body. She spent the next seven months in the hospital and in the years that followed had over 100 surgical procedures. But she did more than just survive. In June 2017, this young woman, then 27 and living in Houston, stepped onto the stage of the TV show *America's Got Talent*. Her name is Kechi Okwuchi, and her singing that night blew the judges, and the audience, away. Kechi doesn't have the outer glamour of a typical star. She'll always carry the scars on her hands, neck, and face of the fire and countless skin grafts. But she revealed another kind of beauty altogether.

In fact, it's what this terrible experience revealed about her that is the true story. Even before *America's Got Talent*, Kechi realized the positive things that came out of this tragedy. First of all, her voice. While her voice was always good, she feels that something happened as a result of the accident, something that made her voice better and stand out a little more—a voice that must be shared. She doesn't know what happened, or why. "I do know that it was not what it is now, compared to what it was before," she said in an interview in 2017.

The second thing that changed was her faith. Before, she saw God primarily through her mother's faith, as a distant entity to be respected and feared. During her hospital stays and long recovery, Kechi developed her own personal relationship with God and began to associate God with pure, unconditional love. God was surely with her, she felt, through some of the most terrible and torturous experiences anyone could endure.

Now, she didn't win *America's Got Talent* that year (she came in sixth), nor did she win in a special series of *AGT: The Champions*, when Simon Cowell gave her the Golden Buzzer for her performance but she failed to make the top five. But the message of Kechi's life came through loud and clear and touched millions: everything she had could have been destroyed, devastated, shaken right

After a tragic plane accident, Kechi Okwuchi began to share her voice with the world.

down to the foundations and never rebuilt, but instead something was stirred in her. Not shaken, but stirred.

In a lighter vein, I once went to see Cher perform in Las Vegas and she told the audience this story about how "Sonny and Cher" became established stars. They had a successful singing career early on but went broke because of some questionable business decisions. They owed the IRS $280,000.

107

The Sonny & Cher star on the Hollywood Walk of Fame.

Sonny came up with the idea to book shows in a dinner club in Toronto. Cher told us it was awful because the chewing and talking noises from the crowd were louder than the band. They were getting discouraged, so Sonny and Cher started teasing each other to ease the tension and keep the band engaged. That experience formed the template for the "Sonny and Cher Show"—Cher as the wise-cracking, glamorous singer and Sonny as the good-natured recipient of her insults. This led to the wild popularity and stardom that would set up the rest of her career.

This life story is not as heavy as the first one, but the principle is the same: what happens to us in our past does not have to define us or limit our future. We can overcome what has happened, and more than that, our past can trigger some new dream, some new hope, some new destiny. What has happened to us can actually stir something in us that takes us further than we ever thought possible.

Thinking about our past is a tricky thing. We nurture all kinds of thoughts and memories. They can seem as real to us today as ever they were long ago. We can hear familiar voices in our heads, smell aromas that take us back to a particular setting or event. It's only in our minds but we are there, experiencing it all over again.

Plenty of these memories are happy and comforting: family life—both our growing-up days and creating our own households as adults—satisfying work, exhilarating travel, encounters with friends, serendipitous moments of every kind. Someone shared with me what he called the shortest short story on record:

"She touched my hand," he said to himself. Actually, she
didn't touch his hand; she brushed his hand by accident while
reaching for the fruit at the grocery. But he said to himself,
"She *touched* my hand." And the memory of that touch stayed
with him through a long and lonely winter.

Many memories are happy, as I say, but often they are of difficult situations, unexpected losses, unwanted transitions, unfulfilled dreams—disappointments, in other words, of every kind and of varying degrees of complexity and duration.

I heard about a man who once had the dream of playing in the Major Leagues. He was almost that good, but not quite. Now in his 50s, he could still see himself out on the diamond in college, smell the fresh cut grass and dirt of the infield, hear the sound of the catcher's mitt when a strike crossed the plate, feel the bat in his hand from a solid base hit. He could be back on the field 35 years ago just like that. But he also relived the agonizing moments of waiting for the call up to the Majors that never came and the ending to each season, including that final one, without ever receiving word that his dream would come true. And now here he is: thinning on top, love handles bulging just a bit more each year over the waistband of his uniform, and being moved down in the batting order yet again to make way for the better hitters on the church softball team.

Our memories can be peculiar and devastating things. The past can seem more real to us than our lives are right now. We can think of particular things from long ago more than we think of the present or future. It can take on a life of its own. William Faulkner wrote, "The past is never dead. It's not even past." It's very much still alive in us right now, in other words. It can become something of an obsession.

Do we even have some notion we know is irrational that we can relive the past somehow and perhaps this time have it turn out better than before? There is that famous line from *The Great Gatsby* where Nick tells Gatsby, "You can't repeat the past." And Gatsby says, "Why of course you can." Gatsby wants to go back to where he once was with Daisy, his one true love, but this time he has wealth and influence so the outcome will be different, he thinks.

He doesn't realize that his obsession with the past has put him on a collision course with the present that will end in disaster. The world has changed, Daisy has changed, everyone and everything around him has changed. Even he has changed. It is only his mind that has remained fixated on recreating the past. "So we beat on," the book ends, "boats against the current, borne back ceaselessly into the past."

We all have to come to terms with the past in our own ways, but at some point there has to be a sense of letting go. We have to stop holding on so tightly to it as if we think we can go back and improve it somehow. We have to give up all hope for a better yesterday. Several years ago, a newspaper reporter interviewed one of the country's best-known psychologists. The reporter asked, "What do you do for those who come to you for treatment?" The noted psychologist answered, "Our objective is to free the patient from the tyranny of the past."

Retired general and former secretary of state Colin Powell tells a delightful story in his book, *It Worked for Me: In Life and Leadership*, about walking down Fifth Avenue in New York City one day when he stopped at a hot dog stand. As the attendant was preparing his hot dog, a look of recognition came across his face. He realized that he knew who this person was; he'd seen him on television, he was famous, but he struggled to pull up his name. Finally, it hit him: "Ah, yes, of course, you're General Powell." Powell acknowledged this and then offered the man the money for the hot dog, but he refused to take it. "No, General, no, you don't owe me anything. I've been paid. America has paid me. I will never forget where I came from, but now I am here. I am an American. I've been given a new life, and so have my children. Thank you, please enjoy the hot dog."

For those of us who can be somewhat obsessed with the past and think of it too often, we have to catch the impact of what this man says. I'm here now. I'll never forget. But now I'm here. Like any immigrant who thinks fondly of the old country but had reasons for making the arduous journey to his new homeland, we too have to understand there are parts of our past that were good and bad, and we won't forget. But now I am here. I have reached a new destination of the present hour. I have been given this time, this moment, this life, and I want to make the most of it.

The road of gratitude is an important one in this context. We have talked about gratitude before, and it's always an important concept. But when we deal with our memories, we are in a territory where gratitude is truly indispensable. If we have good and happy memories, we have to get past the place where we think those days were the very best of our lives, so much better than things are now. Can we be grateful for those days, thank God and the people who were part of our life for helping to shape us in certain powerful ways that have created us as the people we are today? Without those days, we wouldn't be who we are.

Look back, but don't stare, as I heard one person say. Look back every so often, remember, think of the happy times, but don't spend your life there; you have a life right here and now. I love the little phrase, "Don't be sad it's over; be grateful it happened." We have to come to appreciate the present and future more than we do the past.

And if the memories we struggle with are not good and happy, but difficult and troubling, we can still think about them with a sense of gratitude. We can be grateful for the good times that were present even in the midst of the bad, grateful for the character that we were forced to develop, for the friends and family who helped us, grateful to God for a power greater than our own that was ever present. We have become the people we are perhaps even more so because of the bad that has been thrust upon us to overcome or work through.

We should also allow ourselves some time to transition our mind away from the past. It would be nice if we could go through this process of letting go all at once; just say the word to yourself that you are letting this past event or person be hurtled from your thinking and from your life, imagine that it is so, and be done with it. There is the famous story of Robert E. Lee who encountered a woman from the former Confederacy whose family plantation had been decimated by the Yankee army as it marched through.

The mansion was merely a shell and the crops had all been destroyed. But the biggest thing to her was that the old oak tree that had stood on the estate for generations had been reduced cruelly to a twisted and misshapen caricature of its former self. She assumed she had a sympathetic ear in General Lee, so she went on and on about how indispensable that tree had been to her family over the years and how evil the Yankees were.

He let her talk a little, but then finally stopped her and said to her simply, "Madam, cut the tree down and forget it."

Some people are able to just declare that this is no longer going to interfere with your life and forget about it. Or if you need an object lesson to make it more concrete, write your past event or the name of the person who haunts you on a little piece of paper and then throw it away, or burn it, or bury it out in the woods. Maybe you're one who can do this. You should try it and see.

But for most of us, if it's a big enough event in our lives, or person, it takes time and must happen more gradually. We should not be in too much of a rush or too hard on ourselves if we can't just snap our fingers and move on.

Try this: create a time and place in your week to remember the past event that won't seem to leave your mind. Maybe place it on your calendar, schedule an appointment with yourself to think about that one important past experience that you just can't seem to get over. You might even determine a certain location, say, a specific chair in your house or a coffee shop you'll only go to for this purpose. And during that time and in that place, allow yourself to think about this past thing that won't go away. Express your anger and bitterness over it, let it all out, vent your frustrations at people who were thoughtless and cruel. But only allow yourself to think about it at that time and place.

Any other time it comes up in your mind, refuse to think about it. Tell yourself, "I have an appointment on my calendar for that, so I'm going to attend to other things right now." Over time, schedule fewer and fewer appointments with yourself for this. Gradually, it will interfere with your present life less and less.

Powerful memories shape who we are. What we remember and the way we remember are vitally important. If we can see things with a vision that is more hopeful and redemptive, not as having hurt us and held us back but as making room for us to grow and become stronger, we're given a completely fresh and energizing framework for our lives.

There was a story of a little boy whose mother had hands that were pitifully scarred. The boy thought of them as hands that were just so ugly. How could she have gotten such ugly hands? So, one day he asked her why her hands were so ugly. She thought he was old enough now to know, so she told him of the fire in their home when he was just a baby, and how he was trapped in the flames.

Risking her own life, she ran in and plucked him from the fire. But in the process, her hands were burned and scarred forever. The boy was silent for a while, then he took hold of his mother's hands and rubbed them on his face. He looked into her eyes and said, "Mother, you have the most beautiful hands." What we see of our past, and how we see it, determine so much about the way we see our lives in the present.

There is another moving story of a girl who was only ten years old when her father killed himself with a pistol in the bathroom. She came home from school and found him. Her pastor followed this shattered young girl's life closely for four or five years. For the first year, every afternoon at 5:30, he either stopped by her house for a few minutes or called her on the telephone. If he was in a plane, he would write her a note and say, "It is five-thirty. I am here and I wanted you to know that you are not alone." They lost touch after a few years, but 20 years later, when she was in her mid-30s, she came with her mother to visit the pastor. He wrote, "It was a bit of ecstasy to see her grown and effective as a social worker."

She could have remembered the suicide as a penetrating stain on her childhood; she could have dwelt on it and allowed her life to be shaped by the tragedy of what a little girl should never have to experience and could not possibly get over. Or she could think about it as an awful and inexplicable event that happened in her life and brought out the very best in the people around her, including the rare goodness and grace of one particular man, and that helped bring out the very best in her. This second is the path she chose.

I am reminded of two quotes. One is from Sigmund Freud, who wrote, "One day, in retrospect, the years of struggle will strike you as the most beautiful." And the second (and my all-time favorite quote for any occasion), comes from Ray Bradbury, of all people. I've never read a word of Ray Bradbury but somewhere I came across this quote: "Looking back over a lifetime, you see that love was the answer to everything." Love was the one thing, regardless of whatever else was happening all around me and whether I was aware of it or not, that was all the time at work—creating, hoping, healing, making all things new.

Love, grace, and forgiveness are such a huge dimension of this journey out of the deadly and destructive elements of our past. Our lives are full of tragedy, disappointment, hardship, loss. They are all hard to get over, but undoubtedly what we find most difficult to get past are the things other people have done to us: the wounding words, the cruelty, the betrayal. These can loom absolutely monumental in our minds. We can dwell on them, relive them, plot little strategies of getting even.

A reporter from *The New York Times* writes that one of her favorite party games is to ask a group of people this simple question: What is your oldest and most cherished grudge? She says that, without fail, every person unloads with shockingly specific, intimate details about their grudge. Career slights (intentional or not), offhand-yet-cutting remarks, bitter friendship dissolutions—nothing is too small or petty to be remembered.

One of her favorite answers to this question came from a friend whose grudge stretched back to the second grade. A classmate—he still remembered her full name and could describe her in detail—was unkind about a new pair of Coke bottle–thick glasses he started wearing. Her insult wasn't particularly vicious, but he'd been quietly seething about it ever since.

This reminded me of a woman I heard about who was well into her 80s and still remembered the day when she was five and her father gave the biggest ice cream cone to her sister. She had been carrying that around with her all these years. Reese Witherspoon puts it this way as the character Madeline Mackenzie in the HBO series *Big Little Lies*: "I love my grudges. I tend to them like little pets."

Let me ask: Is there a grudge that you are carrying? Anything you are rehearsing over and over in your mind as if you think it may somehow turn out differently this time? Anything you are nurturing to keep it alive, feeding and tending to like a pet, plotting your little scenarios of revenge?

It may be something petty, like these perceived slights with the eyeglasses and ice cream that shouldn't have amounted to much but have lasted decades or lifetimes. They may be very hurtful and real. Someone may have deeply harmed you in some way, either physical damage or ruin to your reputation or career. People can be cruel and thoughtless and take advantage, of you and of those you love.

Is there any possibility that you can eventually—not right away, but eventually—let this go? Is it possible that you could see your way to be able to forgive as the most effective strategy to move on with your life?

I heard of a Jewish man who moved to the United States after World War II and became very successful at what he did. He had been in Auschwitz and had lost most of his family, but he was known as a man who had been able to forgive. Someone asked him once, "How can you possibly forgive the people who did that to you and your family? How are you able to forgive?" And the man said, "I was coming to America. I was coming to a new country. I wanted to start a new life. And I didn't want to bring Hitler and the Gestapo with me to my new life, so I forgave them and left them behind."

It's an understatement to say that this is not an easy thing to do. It was horrendous what happened to this man and millions of others. But I think his story captures perfectly what we are trying to do when we forgive. Forgiveness is really for the person who is forgiving, not the offender. It's about freeing yourself. It doesn't mean that what they did is okay now or that you have to like it. It doesn't mean that you have to become their friend or reconcile with them. All of these things may occur, but they are not the primary functions or outcomes of the action of forgiveness.

Forgiveness means you are letting go of your anger and bitterness and even hatred of the other person for what he or she did to you. What they did will not define who you are any longer. It's enough that someone hurt you when you were five or 15 or 50. Why let them continue to hurt you today? Why should you allow their deeds to control you still, decades later?

There is a classic way of illustrating what happens to us when we can't forgive: holding onto our grudge is like drinking rat poison and waiting for the rat to die. I've also heard it expressed elsewhere as like burning down a house to get rid of the rat. Whatever the metaphor of the grudge, it seems that the rat is always the image of the wrong that gnaws away at us. Failing to forgive is more destructive of us, in other words, than the other person. They may not ever realize or care what they have done, but it can eat away at us, like a poison or toxin, or decimate us like an unquenchable inferno, contaminating and consuming our very soul.

An 1895 photograph of the Richardson Spite House at Lexington Avenue in New York City.

The corner of Lexington Avenue and 82nd Street in New York City has an interesting history. My co-author and his wife lived in that area for a few years when they were first married and walked by that corner practically every day, but they never knew the story. In 1882, a businessman in the city named Joseph Richardson owned a narrow strip of land on that corner that was five feet wide and 104 feet long. Another businessman, Hyman Sarner, owned a normal-sized lot adjacent to Richardson's. He wanted to build apartments that fronted on the avenue, so he offered Richardson $1,000 for the slender plot. Richardson was deeply offended by the amount and demanded $5,000. Sarner thought that was ridiculous and refused. He had wanted to own the five-feet wide parcel so he could extend the apartment building right onto Lexington Avenue. But when Richardson refused to sell at his price, Sarner decided that it really didn't matter whether he had the additional slender piece of land or not. There was no use that Richardson could put to it, he thought, it would have to remain vacant, so

115

the building was designed with the windows of the apartments looking over the vacant land and onto the avenue.

When Richardson saw the finished building, however, he resolved to block the view. No one was going to enjoy a free view over his lot. So, 70-year-old Richardson built an apartment building of his own on the land. It was five feet wide, 104 feet long, and four stories high, with two suites on each floor. Upon completion, he and his wife moved into one of the suites. Only one person at a time could ascend the stairs or pass through the hallway. The largest dining table in any suite was 18 inches wide. A newspaper reporter of some girth once got stuck in the stairwell, and after two tenants were unsuccessful in pushing him free, he could only exit by stripping down to his underwear.

The building was dubbed the "Spite House." Richardson spent the last 14 years of his life in the narrow residence that seemed to fit his narrow state of mind. A few years after he died, in 1915, it was torn down. One can only presume that later developers viewed it as comically pitiful and worthless. Sarner's apartment building was also demolished sometime later. Today, the corner looks nothing like it did at the turn of the twentieth century, which is why my co-author had no inkling of the history.

I had heard about this Spite House from some of my reading and so Googled it to find out more. What I discovered was in some ways unbelievable, because there are all kinds of spite houses that have been built all over the world. I had to wade through many before I came to the one I wanted. It should not have surprised me, though, that a lot of people choose to block the view of a neighbor they don't like or to build where another had hoped to live or expand but didn't offer enough money. An attitude of spite is one way that people do choose to live; I see it all the time. It's just that some have the means to actually put bricks and mortar to their resentment and bitterness.

But when we forgive, we release the poison and hardness of heart. Something new is stirred in us, redeeming or rescuing us to live the life we have been given now. It's no wonder studies reveal that forgiveness reduces stress and depression and has a positive effect on our immune and cardiovascular systems. It takes a lot of energy that has been all pent up to create a building or a life of spite.

Dr. Paul Tournier, well-known in his day as a Swiss physician of spiritual and psychological depth, told in his book *A Doctor's Case Book in Light of the Bible* of treating a woman for anemia. He had been working with her for several months without much success. He had tried all kinds of medicines, vitamins, and diet and exercise, all to no avail. There was no improvement at all. He decided to put her in the hospital as a last resort.

An illustration by Gustave Dore of the Biblical story of Joseph being reunited with his brothers.

However, as she was checking in, the hospital checked her blood as part of the routine. They discovered that she was fine, with no sign of anemia. Dr. Tournier checked her himself and got the same results; she seemed to have been healed miraculously. He asked her, "Has anything out of the ordinary happened in your life since I saw you last?"

"Yes," she said, "I forgave someone against whom I had borne a nasty grudge for a long time. We reconciled. We are friends again. I felt I could at last say 'yes' to life." Her willingness to forgive had a dramatic effect on her physical body.

The story of Joseph and his brothers from the book of Genesis in the Bible gives us an important insight into how our memory can actually help us to forgive.

You may remember that Joseph was the youngest son of Jacob, and his favorite. Jacob gave his son a royal coat of many colors, and often sent him to spy on his brothers, who were jealous and bitter. On one such spying expedition, his brothers turned on him and decided to sell him to passing slave traders headed for Egypt. Several harrowing experiences followed for Joseph and he ended up in prison.

117

Ultimately though, Joseph rises to prominence, second in command to the pharaoh. He is in charge of preparing for the coming worldwide famine and overseeing the distribution of food once it arrives. It is then that his brothers, who sent him to Egypt as a slave, come to find food for themselves and their family. Joseph struggles with what to do. He is tempted to punish them, and he does initially treat them menacingly. But in the end, he forgives them. As he reveals his identity, he utters this astonishing statement, "It was not you who sent me here, but God."

Now, I would submit to you that this is revisionist history, pure and simple; he is misremembering and revising what actually happened. You only need to read a couple of chapters earlier to see that it was the brothers, with intent that was harmful and even evil, who sent him there. It wasn't God, it was them. It's right there in black and white.

Yet with hindsight, by thinking of his experiences as damaging but the eventual cause of so much salvation for so many, Jacob sees God as the lead actor of this whole drama, constantly working to create something good out of what was meant as a disaster. He is not forgetting what happened, just remembering it in a way that gives him a larger and broader perspective of his past.

To Joseph, God is the one ultimately who stirs people to understanding and action when they might have been shaken by their predicaments and circumstances. This gives him the power to forgive, and to forgive completely.

One of the most powerful stories of forgiveness I know had its inception in the Vietnam War. I was fairly young at the time, just 14 when it ended, but I was keenly aware of what was occurring, primarily because of the powerful photography that was coming out of the war. Many pictures caught my attention, but the one I remember most is of soldiers and small children running down a dirt road away from the napalm bombing destruction right behind them. In the middle of the picture was a little girl running, naked, screaming, afraid. I didn't know exactly what happened at the time but the picture, that image of the little girl, stayed with me.

Years later, I learned about the picture and so much more. On June 8, 1972, South Vietnamese airplanes, allied with the United States, dropped napalm bombs on a little village that had been attacked and infiltrated by North Vietnamese troops. A group, mostly children, were running away and were mistaken for the enemy, so more napalm was dropped. Some of her family and neighbors were killed, and Kim Phuc, nine years old, had the clothes burned off of her by the napalm and was covered by third degree burns over 65 percent of her body, a similar proportion of damage sustained by Kechi Okwuchi. The photographer,

Nick Ut, the photographer who shot the famous "Napalm Girl" image, speaks about the photo in 2016.

Nick Ut, who took the famous picture I remember—he won a Pulitzer Prize in 1973 for the photo—saw how badly she was burned and drove her to the nearest hospital. No one expected her to live, but somehow she survived, staying for the next 14 months in the hospital and receiving treatments so painful she would often pass out in the middle of them. For years afterward, Phuc was understandably angry, bitter, and filled with hatred. She was disfigured and in deep emotional and physical pain.

But she began to read the Bible and gradually, over time, she began to see the value of forgiveness to give her hope and a future. Today, Phuc lives in Toronto, Canada, with her husband and two sons. She travels the world telling her story of hope and forgiveness borne out of despair and is a UNESCO Goodwill Ambassador for peace.

Kim Phuc as an adult.

It's not a message everyone is ready to hear. After a presentation she made in Ohio, one woman, who had lost her daughter in the Oklahoma City bombing and was raising her grandchild, stood near the door as Phuc left and angrily confronted her. She could not forgive the bomber and thought it wrong of Phuc to forgive. But Phuc spent time with the woman and told her, "You know what? I can't change what happened in the past. I was nine. I got burned so badly, but what can I do? I never live in the past. I learn from it." After a while, the woman said, "You're right. I'll try it."

On another occasion, Phuc visited a burn unit in Uganda. It was the first time she'd been in such a unit in over 20 years. It brought her back in her mind to the same burn unit she had been in. She felt the same pain and fear. It was a real sacrifice for her to go there. During the emotional visit, she was taken to meet a woman whose husband had thrown acid in her face. The nurse said, "She doesn't want to eat anymore. She doesn't want to live."

Phuc showed the woman her scars. At first, the woman didn't want to hear it. She said, "How can I forgive my husband who did this to me? You can hide your scars with clothes. My scars are so visible. I have a store. No one comes anymore. I have no more friends. I hate him. How can I forgive?"

Phuc told her, "I had the same questions for a long, long time in my life, but I know through experience, God loves me for who I am, not how I look. I trusted God to bring the right people into my life, and he did. Trust God. If you are true, a true friend will come into your life." After a while, the woman listened and began to soften. The nurse saw Phuc later and said, "I'm so thankful you spent time with her. After you left, she stood up. She's smiling. You gave her hope. She doesn't want to die anymore."

Perhaps only someone like Kim Phuc can truly speak at such a deep level about forgiveness, someone who has, because of her past, so much to forgive. But then, we all have a past and a deep level of hurt and pain to forgive. If you're willing, it will certainly be one of the boldest actions you will ever undertake to let go of the past, to remember, but in a way that brings strength and healing and hope and redemption.

STEP SEVEN

What are the strongest memories you have? Do you have one that is powerfully positive and one that is deeply negative? Can you trace yourself from those moments then to where you are now? Can you see how those events or people shaped your life, stirred you in creative and bold directions to become the person you are today? Do you have anything or anyone that you need to forgive? What one step are you going to take today to let go of the bitterness and resentment and move toward forgiveness?

The stands at a University of Alabama football game.

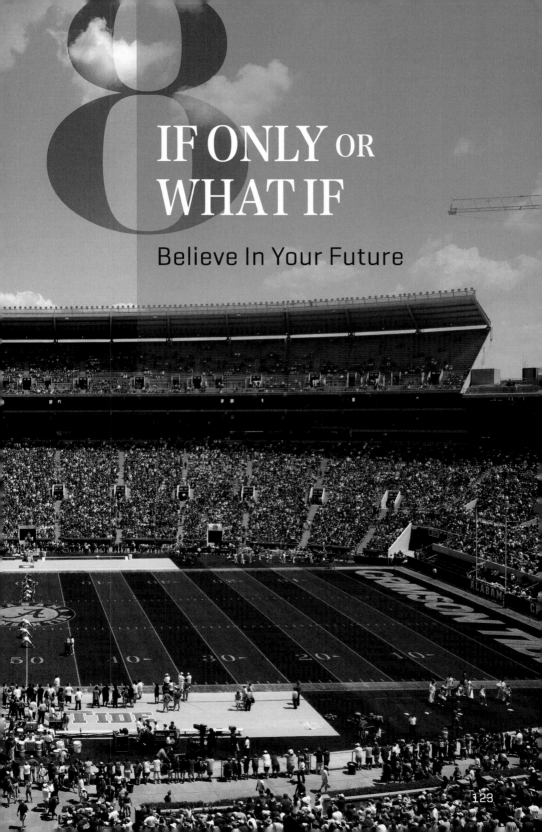

8

IF ONLY OR WHAT IF

Believe In Your Future

In all the annals of resilience and determination and grit, to me nothing quite compares to a specific incident in the life of one particular man. His name was Thomas Carlyle, a Scottish writer of history, philosophy, and social commentary during the Victorian Era of the nineteenth century. Moody or even unhappy in so much of his personal life, his writing was unique and thrilling—"breathless" is the way one person described it, vivid. His historical writings did not just detail events from long ago, they graphically animated lucid moments as they unfurled right before your eyes. One of his first important works, *The French Revolution*, was a three-volume set. When the first volume was published in 1837, it was an immediate success and made his name.

Success and a name, that is, that almost never came. John Stuart Mill, the famous economist and a dear friend of Carlyle's, had helped him financially during the writing of the volume and provided resource material on the subject matter. So, he was understandably interested in reading it as soon as it was finished and begged to see it. Carlyle gave to him, one might imagine somewhat reluctantly, the only copy of the manuscript. (Do you see where this is headed?)

Several days later, Mill came to the door, "pale as Hector's ghost," Carlyle recalled in his memoirs. Mill was absolutely beside himself with apologies as he laid out the lurid tale of the manuscript. He had been reading it late at night, this thoroughly engrossing page-turner, laying each sheet as he finished it on the floor next to his chair, which happened to be situated right next to the fireplace. (If you didn't see it before, do you see where this is headed now?) In the morning the maid, seeing a disorganized jumble of papers, threw the whole pile into the fire. The entire volume was all burned up and gone.

As if the news of this was not enough of a challenge, Carlyle recounts how Mill stayed for three long, mortal hours. He had to pretend to take the matter lightly, so as not to distress his friend too much. He tried to cheer Mill up when all the while, for him, it was like a sentence of death. It had taken years to write that first volume, years filled with poverty and anxiety. He thought of the sheer grind of it all, which had taken its toll on his health and happiness and stolen his youth. The one good thing that came out of this extended time is that Mill told his friend how good the volume was. This writing that now was completely gone had been wonderful, magical, something to behold.

Courageously—I think heroically—Carlyle sat down and wrote the whole volume over again from scratch. The reason I find this story so remarkable is that it would have been so easy to sink into despair and self-pity. It would have been understandable for Carlyle to give up at this point, on that volume or on any volume ever again.

Bronze statue of the historian Thomas Carlyle in Chelsea, London.

He had put everything he had, his whole life, into this project and it had been so carelessly destroyed. He probably did think long and hard about the waste of it all. "I have wasted these years," he must have thought, perhaps over and over, "I have wasted my life. The one good thing I have done is now gone."

Imagine the regret he must have felt. How many times must he have thought, "If only. If only Mill hadn't read it so close to the fire. If only his maid had thought about what she was doing for just a moment longer. If only I hadn't given it to him. I almost said no, he couldn't have blamed me for saying no, if only I had said no."

Instead, at some point, Carlyle must have been able to turn his mind toward a different question: "What if? What if it is as good as I think it is, as good as Mill said it was? What if it changes the way people think about the French Revolution? What if this is an important book that simply must be written? What if I sit down and write it all over again? What if I can make it even better?" I have no proof of this, but I'd like to think that he got started on it that very day, just as soon as Mill mercifully left; there was simply no time to waste.

Where are the "if only" places in your life? Times you regret. Moments you wish you had back. Wistful thoughts you know are impossible of being able to do it over again. Others who took advantage of you, who were thoughtless with your dreams and desires, who let you down. Mistakes, losses, failures, heartbreaks. If only those things hadn't happened.

Sharing the "So what? Now what?" mindset with the University of Alabama football team has helped them overcome hurdles and find new ways to victory.

How can they be turned around so that you begin to ask yourself "What if?" What if I could begin my life over again— or at least an important specific part of it? What if I could have a fresh start from this point on? What if I didn't let what I've done wrong in the past or what others have done to me hold me back from what I could do starting right now? What if I could be healthier, stronger, more committed, bolder? What if I could become the person I've always wanted to be? What would I do now? What would be the first step? What if?

The phrase I often use is "So what? Now what?" I first used it with the University of Alabama football team a couple of years ago. It led to a 25-plus-game winning streak in the 2015-2016 season.

First, you have to ask "So what?" when a door of some kind is slammed on you. I know it almost sounds like you don't care when you say "So what?" or

127

that you're trying to make whatever happened seem like it was unimportant. But that is not the intent. You care deeply; it was very important to you at the time. You wanted that door to be open. But the door is now closed. There is no way to get that burned manuscript back. "So what?" means you are facing the reality that the door is closed and there's no going back. If you make a mistake on the football field, there's no going back to replay the down. If you make a mistake in your life or something happens, someone does something to you, there is no going back; we saw that in the last chapter.

But if you face up to that fact, you enable yourself to begin to ask "Now what?" Now that the door is closed, what am I going to do?

Years ago, a man in Cincinnati, Ohio, named Noah McVicker created a substance that looked like putty or soft clay. His family's soap company marketed his creation as wallpaper cleaner. This putty-like substance was excellent for this because it did not contain any toxic chemicals, could be reused, and did not stain the wallpaper. It was a success and sold well. With all the coal furnaces at the time, wallpaper in homes needed constant cleaning. Sales slowed significantly, however, after World War II when coal was being phased out as an energy source for heating homes, and soon the company was teetering on the edge of bankruptcy. Yet it had all this inventory of the putty-like stuff. What were they going to do with it all?

So what? Now what? One day, this man found out that his nephew's sister-in-law let the children in her classroom play with the putty-like substance, and it gave him an idea. He began to market it as a children's modeling compound for arts and crafts projects and renamed it Play-Doh. It was an immediate success and sold millions the first year. It has now been named one of the 100 most memorable and creative toys of the twentieth century and continues to have tremendous sales all over the world.

If you ever go to Hyde Park, New York, on the Hudson River, you can visit the home of Franklin D. Roos-

The study, with a wheelchair and portrait of Sara Delano Roosevelt, in the FDR Presidential Library & Museum.

evelt, the 32nd president of the United States. You can see his library of thousands of books and samplings of his huge collections of naval paintings and prints, bird specimens, ship models, stamps, coins, and campaign buttons. He was a brilliant and interesting man.

But the part of the tour that made the biggest impression on me came outside the home, when the tour guide took us to a long driveway from the house to the main road. It's about a half mile long. There, the guide recounted what most people know, that Roosevelt contracted polio at the age of 38 and his legs became permanently paralyzed. He was just sure his political career was over. One day, he had this promising future, he'd been the Democratic nominee for vice president the previous year. And the next, it seemed to all have come to an end.

During those dark, uncertain days, the guide told us, Roosevelt would come out with his crutches and try to walk the length of that driveway. The servants would help him out, then retreat to the house because he didn't want them to stay out there with him. They would watch from the front window as Roosevelt would try to walk. With his crutches, he would swing one dead leg over and then the other. Most of the time, he would fall fairly quickly and the servants would

President Franklin Roosevelt at Top Cottage in Hyde Park, New York, with a young girl named Ruthie Bie and his dog Fala in 1941.

come scurrying out to help him up and back into the house, unless he decided to try again. Sometimes he made it a little way, a number of yards; it must have seemed to him at times that he would indeed be able to walk all of the long distance.

But he never did. He never made it.

For most of the decade after he contracted polio, he would go out and try to walk that driveway. Every day. And every day, he fell. Every day, the servants had to come out and carry him back into the house. Every day, he failed in what he set out to do.

He never made it. Not once. He never walked. But he did become the governor of the state of New York. He was elected President of the United States—four times, the most of anyone in history. He did help to free the world from economic depression and the tyranny of fascism.

Roosevelt, I would suggest to you, like Carlyle and the man who invented Play-Doh, believed in his future. It didn't turn out to be the future he must have at first envisioned, where he would walk again. But it was a future that began to form in his mind, maybe with each failed attempt on that long driveway, a future of being a person of worth even with legs that were paralyzed, a future of making an impact of indispensable consequence. The thoughts of "If only" this hadn't happened to me had to begin to turn in a new direction, toward "What if I can still do something that matters with my life?" He had to say to himself, "So what?"—the door I once thought would be open to me has now been closed—and then "Now what?"—what other thing can I set myself to be doing?

You have to believe in your future, even though sometimes you may not know precisely what that future will turn out to be. It may be that the thing you once dreamed would be the future just is not going to happen.

At some point, I had to give up on my dream of playing in the NBA, for example. When I speak to groups of people and say that, I simply have to pause for a moment to let it sink in. For you, I'll complete the picture by telling you that I'm five-foot-nine and not particularly quick. It took me a while to come to the realization that there was no way I was ever going to play in the NBA. But eventually I did.

It was one of many "So what?" moments in my life. But I never gave up on believing in my future. I just had to find what else my future was going to be. I had to begin to ask myself, "Now what?" I had to turn my "If only" into "What if?"

Mark Twain once said, "Twenty years from now, you will be more disappointed by the things you didn't do than by the ones you did do. Sail away from the safe harbor."

Similarly, Walt Whitman wrote in *Leaves of Grass*:

Sail forth – steer for the deep waters only,
Reckless, O soul, exploring, I with thee, and thou with me,
For we are bound where mariner has not yet dared to go,
And we will risk the ship, ourselves, and all.
O my brave soul!
O farther, farther sail!
O daring joy, but safe! Are they not all the seas of God?
O farther, farther, farther sail!

You have to believe in your future; I can't say this often enough, even if you don't know just exactly what it is. You have to believe that, if this, whatever it is that has disappointed you, is not the future, something else will be. You have to believe, as they say, that if one door closes, there must be a window open somewhere. You have to find out what it is. You have to go in search of it. You have to sail away from the safe harbor and into the deep waters.

There has to be a little bit in you of the young boy who was playing left field in a Little League baseball game. A man walked by and noticed the game and started talking to the boy. He asked what the score was, and the boy replied cheerfully that it was 18-0.

The man asked, "Oh, so you're ahead then?" But the boy, again pretty upbeat, said, "No, we're behind." "Well I must say," said the man, "that you don't seem very discouraged." And the boy responded with an innocent look, "Discouraged? Why should I be discouraged? We haven't gotten up to bat yet!"

Now it's true that very few come back from a deficit like that, although if you've ever watched a Little League game with a group of ten-year-old kids, you learn pretty quickly that anything can happen. Maybe this boy had been through this kind of game already in his young life; they'd come back before, so he knew they had a chance. Or maybe it was just the nature of the team that year, terrible pitching but great hitting that allowed them to overcome any deficit. Whatever, for the boy it was just a matter of getting up to bat, having the chance.

For you and me too, a little of this kind of wild innocence can go a long way in any endeavor in which we are engaged. We must begin to believe and live that anything is possible, anything might be accomplished, just give me the chance.

And there has to be a little in you, too, of the old man I heard about who was sitting on a porch in a small town in the middle of nowhere. It was one of those places where you think nothing has ever happened and probably nothing ever will. A stranger came into this small town and saw the old man, so he went over and started talking to him. And the stranger asked, really just making conversation, "What's so special about this little town?" He expected the man to have a hard time coming up with an answer; it didn't seem like there could be anything special about it. But the old man said quickly and confidently, "Why son, from here you can go anywhere you want to in the world."

You have to believe that this is true of your life. Wherever you are presently, there is a future for you. It may seem like you are starting off in the worst place possible to reach a particular destination, maybe even to reach any destination that is worthwhile. You are nowhere, you feel, as you begin. And yet from where you are now, you can go anywhere. You have to be willing to boldly claim that!

There is the story of the little storefront business in Chicago that was totally destroyed by the great fire that occurred there in 1871. It was burned to the ground, everything was gone. But the day after the fire, there was a big hand-made sign that hung prominently from what was left of the building.

It said, "Everything lost but hope. Business will resume as usual tomorrow morning!"

Now, I have to tell you, this boggles my mind. What was he going to sell when the business resumed as usual? I don't know what the business was, but don't you need some inventory or product to actually have any customers? It was all gone, there was nothing left. There was no way that business could resume as usual tomorrow. Except that what may make a business more than anything, even more than having the most original and best product ever invented—especially under that kind of circumstance—is an outlook, an attitude, a certainty, a belief that the business will resume. You think it's so, and work to make it so, until it actually is so.

With your life, you may not know precisely what it will look like tomorrow, but you have to believe in the tomorrow that is coming. No matter what happens to me today, my life will resume as usual tomorrow, or maybe the belief will be that my life will resume tomorrow bigger and better than ever.

Chad Scott played football for the Pittsburgh Steelers when I was a consultant with the team. One day in practice, he tore his ACL, one of the major ligaments in the knee. Head coach Bill Cowher asked me to visit Chad. When I came into the training room, he was on a table and called me over. I asked him how he was dealing with his injury. I'll never forget his response: "I'm chopping down trees and drinking battery acid."

I had to think about that one for a while; he never explained it, but I figure that this is what he meant: if you are chopping down a tree and it doesn't fall, do you quit? Do you tell yourself that you've hit this tree so many times already and it should have fallen by now, so you get discouraged and frustrated because what you expected to happen hasn't happened yet? Do you decide that this is the amount of work that you are going to do, and you will do no more, so you just stop? Or do you keep chopping at that tree until it falls? Well, Chad would say you keep chopping and have faith that you will eventually get there. You believe you have what it takes to stay with it until the end.

I never did entirely figure out what the battery acid reference was all about, except I'm sure it's another way of expressing a never-give-up attitude. Even if there are obstacles in your path, stay with it and believe in your future. You have to stay as tough as you need to for as long as you need to until you get the job done.

It's at just such critical moments in your life when you have to use your imagination. We often don't realize that our imagination is running constantly, 24 hours a day. Taking control of it is the objective. If we're not careful, our imagination can sink us to a real low by allowing our mind to go over and over the bad things that have happened to us, or it can create new scenarios of different failures and disappointments that we tell ourselves are just sure to happen in the future. We've talked about all the negative things that can fill our mind and are very natural for us to cultivate and nurture.

I do love the story of the boy who came home from school one day and told his father that he was sure he had just flunked his math test. And the father said, "Son, don't think like that. You've got to be more positive. You have to think positive." So the boy, trying to psych himself up, said, "Okay Dad, I'll think positive. I'll be positive. I'm positive." But finally, he blurted out, "Dad, I'm positive I flunked that test!" If we don't take command of our imagination, it will most certainly take command of us and take us to the dreariest of places.

But our imagination can raise us to a new high we've never experienced before, too. Of course, our minds may need to be more creative and resourceful than they have ever been. We may have to push ourselves in new directions and toward new ideas.

Part of this progress is simply to continue to grow as individuals who are constantly curious and inquisitive. In 2017, *Time* magazine published a short article, "What 3 Things Can I Do to Extend the Length of My Life?" I expected to read the part about eating more fruit and vegetables, and that was certainly one of the three things. But what I didn't expect was that the first thing mentioned, *the very first thing*, was to "Stay Curious."

"Asking questions and discovering new things keeps you engaged with the world and with other people," the expert interviewed in the article said. Studies reveal that this has longevity benefits because it provides community and hope for the future. Being interested in other people and other things takes us out of ourselves and reminds us that we are part of something far greater than just us and our current circumstances. We are more open and begin to experience what the future might hold when we are curious.

Our imaginations can also enable us to see that things are growing and developing even if it's not always evident on the surface. If you water bamboo for a year, two years, three years, four years, you'll see nothing. Then around the fifth or sixth year, it grows six inches every day above the soil; you can't stop it. You can't see the progress until then, but if you keep watering, the roots are growing underground, establishing a base, preparing the plant for the prolific future that is sure to come. In the same way, when we put a great deal of effort

135

into something but don't see the results right away, we have to continue to believe that something is nevertheless still happening in our lives, something is still at work, something is still developing, something is still growing. Our imaginations can visualize the roots that are gaining strength each day to support what is being created in our life that will one day flourish and grow. If we don't give up but continue to work at it and are patient, something good is being shaped and is coming.

Wherever I speak, I always find a place where I can run or walk or work out in some way. I try to do it every day. I was once in a small town and went over to the high school to walk on the track. It was near the end of summer and school was starting the following week. When I got to the track, there was one paved drive from the street into the small parking lot. I noticed that members of what looked like the cheerleading squad had part of the road blocked off about halfway up the street and were painting something on the surface. It was sketches of the school mascot and words like "Go Team!" and "Fight!" I didn't know how long they'd been there or how far they had gotten that morning, but I knew that sooner or later they would be painting the same things right in front of the only entrance to the track parking lot. I could see faint remnants from where they had painted the same types of images and words in previous years. I was going to be there about an hour, and then needed to get ready for my speaking engagement, so I didn't want to be painted in.

There was another man on the track, about ready to leave, so I asked, "Do you think they'll paint all the way down to the entrance in the next hour? Will I be able to get out?" He assured me that they weren't working that fast. But then he told me that if I did get stuck, I could just drive across the grass to get out; other people did it all the time even when the entrance wasn't closed. When he said that, I realized that the grass was flat; it would be a cinch to drive out that way, I could see tire tracks where others had done it. In fact, once I began to really look and think of how I would get out if I had to, there seemed to literally be an endless stream of possibilities for what I might do to exit the track. I had been so focused on protecting my only way out, the only way I knew, that I hadn't seen all the other possibilities that were really pretty obvious.

This may seem like a small thing, but it woke me up like I really had never experienced before to the fact that once you begin to ask yourself "Now what?" and "What if?" there are endless possibilities out there, a limitless future. Whenever I find myself in a difficult situation where I'm not sure of the next move, and my first reaction is that there may not be a good direction to go or even a way out, I remember that day at the track and I picture once again all the different ways I could have taken that day. I ask myself "Now what?" and "What if?"

and it has always worked; something always is possible, some way is always open. I believe the same will be true for you.

The movie *Gravity* is an intense science fiction thriller starring Sandra Bullock and George Clooney. The two astronauts get stranded in space following the mid-orbit destruction of their space shuttle and attempt to get back to earth. It's a harrowing journey. In fact, the George Clooney character doesn't make it, instead sacrificing himself to save her.

So, Sandra Bullock is alone trying to figure out how to get home and isn't doing very well at first. At one point, she has resigned herself to her fate and shut down the cabin's oxygen supply to basically commit suicide. As she begins to lose consciousness, though, George Clooney suddenly appears. He opens the door to the cabin and climbs in, scolding her for giving up. She tells him that there is nothing that can be done.

But he begins to work some of the controls and says what is, for me, the most pivotal line in the movie: "There's always something you can do." Pretty quickly he is gone again and Sandra Bullock is alone, only now she has begun to figure out for herself what the possibilities are and what she must do. It's a hallucination, of course, a visualization by Bullock of what Clooney might try if he were there and what options are available to her. I won't tell you how it ends, but you must realize that I surely wouldn't have gone through all this explanation of things if it was all over for her in the end.

There's always something you can do. I believe with absolute certainty that if one way is closed to us another way will open. We have to ask ourselves "Now what?" and "What if?" until we find the way. We might not only discover a different way, but one that is so much more important and compelling of a direction, one with even greater meaning and purpose, a direction we realize now that we simply must go. We had never even considered this as a way that was open for us before a door closed and we began to ask ourselves those questions that inevitably point us in a new and promising direction.

I've heard this expressed in a way that I think is memorable and beautiful. It was spoken by a man who had experienced the death of someone very close to him. But he realized that even as tough as this loss was, he was learning and growing from it. He said, "There is always another side to things, a mystery. No matter how great the loss, something else is also true."

There was a young, inexperienced teacher in New York City whose job was to visit children in the hospital to help them keep up with their studies until they could return to school. One morning, she got the name of a boy who needed help with his nouns and verbs. She went to the hospital and discovered that he was in the burn unit.

She wasn't prepared for the sight of a badly burned boy, wracked with terrible pain. But this was her job, so she went in and blurted out something about being his teacher there to help him learn verbs and nouns. Well, the lesson did not go well at all. The little boy was uncomfortable, finding it hard to concentrate. The teacher was even more uncomfortable, wondering if she was the right person for this kind of job, sick at the sight of his condition, fumbling at everything she said and did. The whole lesson was something of a disaster.

But she went back the next day, and as she was coming in, a nurse came up to her and asked, "What on earth did you do to that boy?" She was about to apologize for her poor performance that must have upset the vulnerable child; it must have been even worse than she thought. The nurse went on to say, "We've been very worried about him, but ever since you were here yesterday, his whole attitude has changed. Now he's fighting back, responding to treatment. For whatever reason, he's decided to live." The boy explained later, after he left the hospital, that he had indeed given up hope, he had completely given up—until he saw the teacher. As she stood fumbling but earnest at the foot of his bed, he said to himself, "They wouldn't send a teacher to work on verbs and nouns if I were dying, would they?" It was all he needed to find his footing in the hopeful world of the future.

Just that littlest spark of knowing what the possibilities are, knowing that there are indeed possibilities, may make all the difference and open up the floodgates. There is always something you can do.

Something else is also true. I've mentioned that I often speak to the University of Alabama football team, and I close with the same story every time. It happened at school when I was a boy. Two other boys were going to fight after school one day, and honestly, I couldn't wait to see it. But this fight was quick. One boy shoved the other one down a hill and that was that. At least, that's what we all thought; that's the way it appeared.

The gathered crowd all started to walk back to the school building. But the boy who everyone thought was defeated came up over the hill with a tree branch in his hand and said, "Wait a minute! Where is everyone going? This fight is not over . . .," then he said one of my favorite words: "yet."

The word *yet* is one of the most powerful we have at our disposal, because it shows we believe in the future and what is happening now is anything but final.

We saw that word earlier with the boy who hadn't gotten up to bat yet. And I heard it expressed comically when a man in his 80s was asked by an acquaintance who was making perfunctory inquiries to try to get to know him better, "Do you have any children?" And the octogenarian, with a mischievous twinkle in his eye, answered, "Not yet!" This may be carrying it a bit too far, but the principle is the same: you have to believe regardless of the circumstances. There is a future no matter what is happening in the present.

So where are you with regard to the future? When something happens—a failure, a disappointment, a setback, a loss— and a door has closed, there's no denying it. There's no going back. Something is definitely over and finished. But can you see as well that the door closing is anything but final?

The fight is not over yet. Can you begin to ask the questions that will open up other possibilities, maybe possibilities that open up your life to big and meaningful things you might never have thought were available to you at all? *So what? Now what? What if?* Can you ask those questions that will create a belief in your future and give you a future in which to believe?

STEP EIGHT

What is the biggest "If only?" in your life right now? Brainstorm the "What ifs?" that provide an alternative future. Take out a sheet of paper and write them all down—put down everything you can think of. Do this for every "If only?" you have. Say to yourself, "So what? Now what?" whenever you encounter an obstacle or impediment. Do this even if it's something small, so that it becomes ingrained and second nature. Remember the phrases, "There's always something you can do" and "Something else is also true." And don't forget to insert the word *yet* into your thinking and speaking whenever you're tempted to give up.

Wilma Rudolph at the finish line during a 50-yard dash at a Madison Square Garden track meet.

SPENDING OR INVESTING

Believe In Others

Let me tell you about a little girl who was born into a very poor family in the backwoods of Tennessee. She was the 20th of 22 children, prematurely born and frail. Even her survival was in doubt at first.

When she was four years old, she developed double pneumonia and scarlet fever, which left her with a paralyzed and useless left leg. She had to wear an iron leg brace. Yet, she had a mother who encouraged her and told her that, if she put her mind to it, she could be anything she wanted to be, do anything she wanted to do.

At the age of nine, against doctor's orders, this little girl took off her leg brace and took her first feeble step. It took her four years, but finally she began to walk almost normally.

Then she got this crazy notion that she wanted to be a runner—she wanted to be the world's fastest woman runner. At age 13, she entered a race. She came in last, dead last—way last. She entered every race in high school, and in every one, she came in last.

Everyone but her mother begged her to quit.

She kept at it, and there came the day when she didn't come in last; she came in next to last. Then, one day she won.

From then on, Wilma Rudolph won every race she entered. She went to the 1960 Olympics and won three gold medals, the first American woman to do so. One of the races was a relay where she dropped the baton, had to go back for it, and—unbelievably, impossibly—she caught up with the other runners and won.

I could have used the life story of this great runner in just about any chapter of this book. Wilma certainly believed in the vision she had for her life. She literally took one step after another in pursuit of her goal and overcame some of the most devastating obstacles that can be imagined.

I could go on, describing her personal strength in every area we have discussed so far. But the reason I am placing her story here is that Wilma Rudolph was once asked by a reporter what helped her to overcome her early illnesses and all the impediments. She said, "Well, many people told me I would never walk again. My mother told me I would. I believed my mother."

It was her mother, constantly planting words of affirmation, encouragement, and inspiration into her mind, who helped her create a life of such accomplishment and consequence.

Paul "Bear" Bryant, the famous former head coach of the University of Alabama football team, used to tell his players and others, "Call your Momma, because I sure wish I could." His mother had passed away, and he could no longer communicate with the one person who had the biggest influence on his life. When

Wilma Rudolph at the 1960 Olympics.

he was asked why he returned to Alabama to coach, he replied, "Momma called. And when Momma calls, you just have to come runnin'."

I feel very much the same way about my mother. She was a strong person who gave me a great gift: she believed in me. No matter what was happening to me or what doubts I may have had about what I should do, I always knew there was one person in the world who believed in me. I miss her, and can still hear her say, "I never worry about Kevin because I have faith in him."

I owe so much to her belief in me and, like Wilma Rudolph and Bear Bryant, literally do not know where I would be without her.

Maybe you feel the same. Or maybe it was a father who was most instrumental in your development. Toni Morrison is one of my favorite writers of fiction. She won the Nobel Prize in Literature for her body of work. At the press conference, she was asked who mentored her to help bring her to this place of honor. "What professor in your past helped you get here?" She responded, "It was not a mentor or professor. It was the way my father's eyes lit up every time I walked into the room."

Our parents have this indispensable place in our memories and in our lives. Theirs were the first faces we saw above our cribs, theirs the hands that picked us up when we fell, the arms that held us close when we were afraid. I know not everyone has had decent parents. Some of you reading this may not even have had parents that you could really call a mother or father. But I pray there has been someone who lit up when you came into a room, who encouraged you and invested in you, who created a sense of expectation about what your life could become.

There is a legendary story of a little boy who was taken by his mother to a concert by the great Ignacy Paderewski, the famous Polish pianist and composer. Before the concert began, the boy slipped away from his mother when she wasn't looking, made his way to the stage, sat down at the grand piano, and began to play "Chopsticks." When people in the crowd noticed, they were horrified and angry and began to call loudly for someone to take the boy away. His mother, embarrassed beyond words, was frantically trying to get up onto the platform to pull him away from the piano and back to his seat.

But before she could get there, Paderewski, having heard the commotion, came out onto the stage and walked up behind the little boy. He reached around him and began to play little tunes that harmonized with and complemented the "Chopsticks" the boy continued to play. It became an unrepeatable, improvisational concert the crowd would not soon forget. And all the while, Paderewski was whispering in the boy's ear, "Keep going. Don't quit, son. Keep playing. Don't stop. Don't quit."

None of us has probably been in a situation quite like this, but what is our response, who comes to mind, when we ask ourselves: Who has encouraged me when everyone else was saying I should quit or it couldn't be done? Who believed in me when no one else did? Who has planted words of confidence and expectation deep into my mind and heart?

Max Lucado, the minister and inspirational writer, shares a story from a friend who had just returned from Disney World. He and his family were inside Cinderella's castle, which was packed with children and parents. Cinderella was a gorgeous young girl with each hair in place, flawless skin, and a beaming smile—absolutely perfect for the role. When she entered the room, all the children rushed over to her. She stood waist-deep in an undulating sea of children, each wanting to touch and be touched.

Cinderella's Castle at Walt Disney World.

The friend who told Lucado this was standing there, taking it all in, when he glanced in the other direction and saw a boy, maybe seven or eight years old, standing there. His age was hard to determine because of the disfigurement of his body. Dwarfed in height, face deformed, he stood watching quietly and wistfully, holding the hand of an older brother.

It doesn't take much to imagine what he wanted: to be with the other children. He must have longed to be in the middle of the kids reaching for Cinderella, calling her name. But the fear was understandably too much: fear of yet another rejection, fear of being judged and taunted—again.

The man wished Cinderella would go over to the little boy, but it seemed so unlikely. He couldn't quite believe it when she did. She noticed the boy and almost immediately began making her way in his direction. Politely but firmly, inching through the crowd of children, she finally broke free.

When she reached him, she knelt at eye level with the stunned boy, speaking to him, holding his hand. His face was radiant and transfigured as she leaned in and placed a kiss on his cheek.

This story brings a tear to the eye, doesn't it? Again, perhaps we have not experienced anything quite like this ourselves, either as the man watching or as the little boy, but can you see this vulnerable and impressionable boy as a metaphor for our own lives in some way? Who noticed me when everyone else ignored me? Who touched my life and gave me hope when there was no one else? Who walked into my life when the rest of the world had walked out?

There was a young man who was just starting out in the ministry at his first church. He was pretty green and inexperienced. Nevertheless, he thought he had his work as a minister pretty well figured out; he'd done well at a good seminary and was known as a powerful communicator in the pulpit.

Yes, young as he was, he assumed he knew what to do as the leader of the church—until the phone rang one morning unexpectedly. The father of his board chairman had died without warning. As he started to the family's house, it hit him: "I don't know what to do. I'm their pastor and I'm scared. I don't know what to say to them."

He tried to remember his classes on pastoral care, tried to recall appropriate Bible passages to quote, tried to think of some profound theological message to give these people in their shocked hour of need.

He plotted his strategy: "I know what I'll do. I'll go in boldly and take charge. I'll gather all the family in the living room and quote the 23rd Psalm. That's what I'll do. That's the answer!"

But there was one thing he had not counted on. When he got to the home and gathered the family in the living room, he looked at their faces, and their pain became his pain. He suddenly realized how much he loved these wonderful people, and his heart broke with theirs. He was overcome with emotion.

He tried to quote the 23rd Psalm, beginning, "The Lord is my shepherd …," but he exploded into tears. He cried so hard the family had to rush over and help him. They walked him over to the couch, mopped his brow with a cold cloth, and brought him a glass of water.

The young minister was so humiliated, so ashamed. He felt that he had failed miserably. Somehow he got through the funeral, but he always tried to avoid the family after that; it embarrassed him, and he was sure they must be laughing at him as a total amateur who was incompetent at his job. As luck would have it, the bishop transferred him shortly after this, which was kind of a relief; at least he would not have to face that family again.

Several years passed, and he had to be back in the vicinity of his first church. He thought of that family as he drove into town. It seemed unlikely that he would run into them, but as he was walking around town and turned a corner, who should he walk into but a couple members of this family. The embarrassment and shame came back immediately.

But their reaction was the exact opposite of what he was expecting. Their faces became animated when they saw him. They ran to him and hugged him warmly. "Oh," they said, "we are so glad to see you! Our family loves you. We appreciate you so much. We miss you. We talk about you all the time. We have loved all of our pastors, but you are the one we loved the most!"

"Oh really?" the minister asked with genuine surprise. "Oh yes!" they said. "We'll never forget how you came and cried with us when Daddy died."

You never know, you may entirely misjudge the situation and effect you have on other people. Being present with them, especially in their hour of need, is so much more important than knowing precisely what to do and say. So, allow me to ask once again: Who has been there for you when you were in need? Who has come running at a moment's notice? Who has cried with you? Who has shared the burden of what you are going through?

I think it is powerful to bring to mind those people who have had the biggest positive influence on our lives, people who have been there for us, people we could count on, people who wanted the best for us, who were willing to invest something of their lives in us. I can think of so many: parents, family, friends, ministers, teachers, co-workers, neighbors, people I didn't even know who happened to be there and were willing to extend themselves and help me in some way. Knowing people care can affect the course of a person's whole life.

Remembering their names and faces and what they did for us helps us to remember that we are people of worth, that there is greatness in us, that we have a purpose and destiny. We know this because others have seen it in us and expressed their confidence in us and support for us.

We need each other. We need the relationship and connection of other people in our lives. In my opinion, this is a deep and enduring truth that almost goes without saying. And yet, I know so many who think they have gotten to where they are on their own, who think they can do it all by themselves and don't need anyone else.

The best and funniest illustration that demolishes this idea that we can do it on our own is about a famous organist in the 1800s. He would travel from town to town giving concerts. These were the days when someone had to work behind the scenes to pump the organ while the musician played the keys, so in each place the organist hired a boy to pump the organ during the concert. In one town, he hired a precocious boy who continued to hang around with him even afterward. He couldn't shake the boy, who followed him to his hotel. "We sure had us a great concert tonight, didn't we?" the boy said at one point. "What do you mean we?" said the musician. "I had a great concert. There is no we. There is only I. Now why don't you go home?" So, the boy went home.

The next night, though, when the organist was halfway through a magnificent fugue, the organ suddenly stopped. It gave a little groan, then just quit. The organist continued to play for a few seconds, but there was absolutely no sound. He was stupefied and didn't know what to do; nothing like this had ever happened before. What could possibly be wrong?

Just then the little boy stuck his head around the corner, grinned, and said, "We aren't having a very good concert tonight, are we?"

This story is kind of preposterous, which suits me because I think it is just as preposterous for anyone to think that you can do it on your own. I don't know of a single self-made person—not one. Everyone I have ever known who has come to some measure of success has had the help of at least one person along the way. The poet and dean of St. Paul's Cathedral in London, John Donne, put it this way:

> No man is an island,
> Entire of itself;
> Every man is a piece of the continent,
> A part of the main.
> If a clod be washed away by the sea,
> Europe is the less,

As well as if a promontory were:
As well as if a manor of thy friend's
Or of thine own were.
Any man's death diminishes me,
Because I am involved in mankind.
And therefore never send to know for whom the bell tolls;
It tolls for thee.

Now I know there are some—maybe you're one—who came from absolutely nothing and have worked hard and reached a position of some substance. No one could look at you and see anything other than a huge success. You are justifiably proud. There is an inner strength in you. Many of the steps in this book are designed to help any person grasp some core understandings that will make you bolder in believing in yourself, your vision, and your own resilience. I congratulate you because you have obviously mastered so many of these basic attitudes and skills.

But if you look just a little deeper into the twists and turns of your life and what has happened to you along the way, I wonder if you will not find someone else there as well. Someone who gave you a chance, someone who hired you, who opened a door, encouraged you, guided you, challenged you, inspired you, trusted you, believed in you. You might have had the skill and the aptitude already, you were ready to make the most of the opportunity, and you have indeed worked harder and sacrificed more than you ever thought possible. It has taken a lot of you to get where you are.

I have no doubt, however, that it has taken help from others to get you there as well. I wonder if you have to really think all that hard before the faces come to mind of those who have been absolutely indispensable to you on your journey. Yes, my guess is there was someone there for you, maybe many someones, probably someone at every critical turning point. They have helped to make you who you are, too!

So, let me repeat: We need other people. We can't do it on our own.

We need to say this periodically and experience it; it makes us stronger when we do so. I remember seeing a sermon title for the July Fourth weekend one year: "Celebrating Our Declaration of Dependence." There is strength, the minister was saying, in recognizing and declaring the power of connection and relationship. The presence of other people in our lives raises us to a new level.

Someone was describing a symphony orchestra, at first talking about each individual instrument. By itself, each one can make a beautiful sound and melody. By themselves, they make music. But together, this person said, they make magic.

Similarly, I remember a quote from Misty May-Treanor, half of the unbelievable beach volleyball team with Kerri Walsh Jennings that won three Olympic gold medals. After their second win in 2008, I heard an interview with Misty when she said, "You know, by ourselves, we're good volleyball players. We're pretty good. We are certainly above average." Then she said, with a little twinkle in her eye, "But together we're invincible!"

There is a power in recognizing that we complement each other in our efforts. To have the possibility of going from above average, or even average, in what you do alone to invincible when you're with someone else is no small thing. We have the ability to raise each other to new heights.

As someone has said, "None of us is as strong as all of us." I agree wholeheartedly with this statement. In fact, I think you could take out the word strong and put any number of words in its place: smart, talented, brave, determined, resilient, daring. There is strength in the numbers that combine to reach for any great thing. None of us is as hopeful as all of us.

Misty May-Treanor and Kerri Walsh Jennings know when they play together, they're "invincible."

We all know that geese fly in a V formation. They do this for two important reasons. First, it conserves their energy. Each bird flies slightly above the bird in front of him, resulting in a reduction in wind resistance for the one following. The birds take turns being in front, falling back when they get tired. In this way, the geese can fly for longer periods of time before they must stop for rest. By flying this way, they can glide more often and reduce energy expenditure. The second benefit of flying in V formation is that it is easy to keep track of every bird in the group. It assists with the coordination and communication within the group. Fighter pilots often use this formation for the same reason. We can fly further and faster, too, toward our goals and objectives when we fly together.

I am intrigued by an old anecdote that occurred at a state fair in the Midwest. Spectators had gathered for an old-fashioned horse pull. Various weights were placed on a horse-drawn sled to see which horse could pull the most. The grand champion pulled a sled with 4,500 pounds on it, and the runner up was close with a 4,400-pound pull. Some of the people wondered what the two horses could pull if hitched together, so they decided to try it out.

Separately they had totaled slightly under 9,000 pounds, but when they worked together as a team, they pulled over 12,000 pounds. My father used to always say, "One plus one equals more than two." I have gradually over the years come to understand what he meant.

Former Chicago Bulls center Stacey King.

One of my heroes in sports is Michael Jordan, who played in the NBA for the Chicago Bulls, leading them to six championships. He averaged over 30 points per game, and in one spectacular evening in 1990, he scored a career-high 69 points. Stacey King, a rookie that season and a very good player (albeit primarily in a supporting role), had scored only one point that night. But when asked about the game, he said, "I'll always remember this as the night Michael and I combined to score 70 points!"

As a minister of many years, my co-author has observed, and sometimes sung with, choirs of all sizes and rank, and he will tell you that you need those one or two people who can raise the level of part or all of your musical ensemble. He remembers especially a tenor in one choir who could change the tone and quality of the whole choir when he was present. Other men who had good voices but couldn't read music quite as well or weren't as sure of themselves didn't sing too loudly when it was just them, but they would suddenly sing in full voice and in nearly perfect pitch as they followed his lead. It was amazing to listen as the whole choir, men's voices and women's, began to reach for, and achieve, a sound and harmony and timbre they could never hope to have on their own.

Admiral William McRaven describes in his book, *Make Your Bed*, one segment of his training to become a Navy SEAL. It was during Hell Week, when he and the others in that year's class encountered the mudflats, an area between San Diego and Tijuana where the water runs off and creates a swampy patch where the mud will engulf you. There they were for 15 hours trying to survive the freezing cold mud, the howling wind, and the incessant pressure from the instructors to quit.

The mud consumed each man until there was nothing visible but their heads. As the sun began to set and there were eight more hours of bone-chilling cold until it came back up, it was apparent that some were about to give up. The chattering teeth and shivering moans of the trainees were so loud it was hard to hear anything else.

And then, one voice began to echo through the night—one voice raised in song. It was terribly out of tune but sang with great enthusiasm. One voice became two and two became three and before long everyone in the class was singing. They knew that if one could rise above the misery, others could as well. The instructors threatened them with more time in the mud if they kept up the singing, but the singing persisted. And somehow the mud seemed a little warmer, the wind a little tamer, and the dawn not so far away.

There is a power that is available to us when we recognize the strength and determination and courage that others can give to us. People can uplift us and enlarge us and take us to another level.

But I think the real strength and power comes when we recognize the value of the contribution we can make to the lives of other people. We can enlarge and uplift other people and help them rise to another level. It simply takes an investment of our lives in another person, the way someone has invested—and no doubt continues to invest—in us. We are not just spending our time; we are investing our time, we are investing our lives.

Someone asked, "How do you spell love?" The answer: "Well, you spell it T-I-M-E." We need to take time to touch the lives of other people just as others have touched ours.

153

It doesn't necessarily take a lot of time, either. We can help others in small, simple ways. My co-author was once at McDonald's with his wife, and they waited in line to order behind two young women who were probably in their late teens or early 20s. When they got up to the counter, they noticed one of the young women had left her purse behind. So, he gently walked over to where they were at the drinks counter and softly said, "I think one of you may have left your purse up at the counter." When he said this, one of the young women saw the purse lying there and walked over to retrieve it.

She thanked him, all the while looking at him in amazement, like she'd never seen anyone return a purse before. When she got back with her friend, she exclaimed, "These people are awesome!" He told me later, "I don't know about you, but it's not all the time that people tell me that I'm awesome." And yet he was awesome in a very real way, contributing a little effort to make the world a better place, as corny as that sounds, and helping those impressionable young women feel that the world is a place where people can be trusted. It only took a minute, but he deposited a little emotional investment in the life of another person.

It made him remember one of his churches, where there had been a thriving youth ministry. As the minister, he was always eager to assist the youth as they went on their annual mission trip to help others, often people of real need. He wanted the church to instill values of service and sacrifice in their young minds and hearts.

One year, for an international mission trip to Nicaragua, the youth director came up with the idea of investment certificates, sort of like a stock certificate. Anyone who invested a certain amount of money in the mission trip received a dividend of coming to a special dinner hosted by the youth, where they would tell all about the trip, what they had done for people, and what they had learned. In many ways, it was a fundraiser pure and simple, like a car wash or spaghetti dinner or bake sale. But it turned out to be so much more than that.

At one point while announcing it, referring obliquely to the downturn in the economy at the time, he said, "This may be the best investment many of us are going to make this year." And it was, to many of the people of the church, an investment they were making in the lives of their young people. He doesn't remember how many came up to him and said that they liked thinking of it as an investment, and the dividend was not the dinner (as tasty and wonderful as it was); it was going to be paid down the road as the teenagers grew and matured and carried the memory of their experience with them into every endeavor and vocation. The adults who supported them may never see the ultimate results of their investments, although they did see the first yields in the homes that were built for families who had been living essentially on the Managua city garbage dump. It totally changed the lives of those children, and it wholly transformed the lives of the young people of the church, too.

It really does, I believe, take a village, to raise a child and support and encourage and strengthen one another. It takes a family, it takes a community, it takes a church, it takes a group (just about any group), it takes a person (just about any person) who is willing to invest something of himself or herself in the life of another. It takes someone exactly like you and me to get it started and keep it going.

It's powerful to see yourself as the recipient of such a gift. Just think, you were worth someone else's investment! And it's powerful to see yourself begin to make such an investment. Someone else is worth your investment in them! Just as I have encouraged you to think back on those who have invested in you, can you look around and see those in whom you might invest? Can you see yourself begin to understand and repeat this pattern? Can you see how this has shaped your life and how you might now begin to shape others?

Who connected with me? With whom can I connect?

Who touched my life in a positive way? Who can I touch in a positive way?

Who challenged and inspired me? Who can I challenge and inspire?

Who planted words of affirmation and encouragement in me? In whom can I plant words of affirmation and encouragement?

Who saw something special in me? In whom can I see something special?

Who believed in me? In whom can I believe?

Who helped raise me to a new level? Who can I help raise to a new level?

Look for that person, and after you've done it once, do it again. See how many people's lives you can touch. Go out of your way. Get out of your comfort zone. They are worth it, just like you were once worth it to someone else. Continue the pattern. Help shape others' lives the way others shaped yours. Invest in others the way others have invested in you.

Sister Helen Mrosla was a teacher at Saint Mary's School in Minnesota. A special teacher, she was not only skillful in the classroom, she was thought of by her students as one who genuinely cared about them. Sister Helen was teaching third grade one year and had one student, Mark Eklund, who she thought of as "one in a million." He was smart and handsome and always neat in appearance, but it was his carefree attitude and mischievous nature that stood out. And it seemed like he was always talking incessantly in class. Quite often, Sister Helen had to remind Mark that talking without permission was not acceptable. Every time she did, Mark would say sincerely, "Thank you for correcting me, Sister." She got accustomed to hearing that many times a day.

One day, when her patience grew thin and Mark talked once too often, she even threatened to tape his mouth shut if he kept it up, which, of course, he did. So, she took out a roll of masking tape, tore off two pieces, and made a big X over Mark's mouth. When she returned to the front of the classroom, she glanced at Mark, and he winked at her. Well, she couldn't help herself and started laughing. The whole room laughed and cheered, and she soon removed the tape. "Thank you for correcting me, Sister," Mark said immediately.

The next year, Sister Helen was asked to teach junior high math, so a few years later, she had Mark in her classroom again. He was not as much of a chatterbox now, but still as handsome and mischievous as ever. One Friday, things just did not feel right in the classroom for some reason; something was off. The students had worked hard all week on a new math concept and seemed edgy and cranky. Sister Helen felt she needed to do something completely different, something that had nothing to do with math, to get her students in a better frame of mind.

So, she asked them to list the names of each of their classmates in the room, think of the nicest thing they could say about each one, and write it down. This took the rest of the period and the students handed their papers to her as they left for the weekend. As he left, Mark said to her, "Thank you for teaching me, Sister." Over the weekend, Sister Helen compiled what her students had written, writing down the name of each student on a separate sheet of paper and then listing what everyone else had said about that individual. On Monday, she gave each student his or her list, and it immediately changed the whole atmosphere.

As they read down their lists, you could hear comments like, "I never knew that meant anything to anyone," and "I didn't know others liked me so much." No one ever mentioned those papers again in class after that day, but the mood in class seemed friendlier and happier for the rest of the semester.

The years went by, and one day Sister Helen learned that Mark had been killed in Vietnam. She hadn't heard from the family or seen Mark in a long, long time, but his parents wanted her to come to the funeral. As she looked at him in the casket, it seemed unreal that Mark, who had been so young and so fine and so full of life, could be gone. She thought, "I'd give all the masking tape in the world if Mark would talk to me now." At the gathering of family and friends after the funeral, Mark's mother and father were there, waiting for Sister Helen.

"We want to show you something," his father said. He pulled out a wallet. "This is Mark's. They found it on him when he was killed. There's something in here that I think you will recognize." Opening the billfold, he carefully removed two worn pieces of notebook paper that had been taped and folded and refolded many times. Sister Helen knew immediately what it was: the list of all the good things Mark's classmates had said about him way back in junior high. "Thank you so much for doing that," Mark's mother said. "As you can see, Mark treasured it."

Then something really amazing happened. Mark's former classmates had gathered around. One, Charlie, blurted out, "I still have my list! It's in the top drawer of my desk at home." Another, Marilyn, said, "I have mine too. It's in my diary." One classmate's wife said, "Chuck asked me to put his list in our wedding album, and I did." Vicki, still another, reached into her purse, took out her wallet, and showed her worn and frayed list to the group. "I carry my list with me at all times. I think we all saved our lists."

Sister Helen, who had been quite stoic throughout the funeral, finally began to cry—for Mark and those who would miss him, and because she was so touched that they had all kept their lists from that day.

There is a power, a boldness, that comes to us when we recognize our need for and dependence on others, the contribution to and investment in our lives that they have made and continue to make. And I believe there is an even greater power and boldness that comes from the contribution and investment we can make in the lives of others to help shape them and mold them into something genuine and great.

STEP NINE

Who are the people who have had the most influence and impact on your life? Can you remember their names? See their faces? How does it make a difference in your mind to perceive that they were not just spending time with you but making an investment in you? Who are the people in whom you are going to make an investment? Write down their names, along with one or two actions you are going to take.

The Golden Gate Bridge.

10

SUCCESS OR SIGNIFICANCE

Believe In Your Impact

On the morning of September 25, 2000, when 19-year-old Kevin Hines looked out from the Golden Gate Bridge, it must have been a magnificent sight. The sun bouncing off the coastline of Marin County to the left and backlighting the city of San Francisco to the right, with Alcatraz Island straight ahead. There were probably boats of different types and sizes in the glittering water and an occasional sea lion breaking the surface. The Golden Gate Bridge is one of the world's most exquisite, an American landmark.

Despite that—or perhaps because of it—it has also been one of the most infamous places in the world for people to die by suicide. It was on this stunning bridge on this perfect day that Kevin Hines decided to jump.

The 220-foot fall takes only a few seconds but probably feels a lot longer. By the time you hit the water, having accelerated to 80 miles per hour, the surface of the water functions more like concrete and does similar damage to the body. Spinal vertebrae and the thoracic ribcage snap like twigs and then rip through the organs in the abdomen and chest. Arteries and veins tear open and the body's cavities fill with blood. The pain is searing, and as you plunge into the frigid water, you are likely to drown—if you are even still alive.

As soon as Kevin's hands and feet left the bridge, he felt "instantaneous regret." He tried to maneuver his body so he could land feet first, knowing that would be his only chance of survival. Somehow, miraculously, it worked.

Sanjay Gupta of CNN interviewed Kevin 19 years later, as the nets on the bridge were finally going up to prevent other falls or suicides. This was a day for which he had long advocated. All this time later, Kevin seemed to have healed completely and bear no external scars. He appeared perfectly fine and fit and healthy.

You have to look deeper and read the X-rays that show the titanium cages holding his spine together to see the damage.

Similarly, you need to look deeper to see that this is not just a tale of survival, it is about empathy, compassion, and our basic human obligations to one another.

Kevin Hines is a suicide prevention activist and shares his own story about how his attempt to end his life led to him learning how to truly live.

160

On that day in 2000, Kevin walked from his home to the bus stop, rode to the Golden Gate Bridge, and then walked to the middle of it. What no one he encountered knew was that he had made a silent pact with himself: if anyone offered him a kind word or "friendly eyes," as he called them, he wouldn't jump. He just wanted to see one act of compassion in a city full of people to convince this obviously troubled 19-year-old kid that he should live.

But on that day, no one rose to the occasion. That part of the story still tears at him and at times cripples him. Of all the people he passed that day from his home to the bridge, not one person smiled or said, "Hello," or asked, "How are you?"

We could just chalk it up to a big impersonal city where people don't know their neighbors, much less care about them, or care about anyone they don't know, for that matter. It's a jungle out there and you'd better be concerned about number one because no one else will. That's the stereotype of people in a big city, I suppose. And they sure lived up to it that day.

But let me ask you sincerely (and please answer honestly, you're the only one who will ever know): if Kevin had walked past you that day and all he needed was a smile, would he have jumped off that bridge or would he have gone back home with a sense of hope? What expression do you wear on your face? What attitude do you offer the world? Are we all too busy and preoccupied and stressed out and, frankly, self-centered, to notice or care about anyone else but ourselves and our family and a small group of friends? If all it took was a face that was friendly and warm for a person you didn't know at all, who was hanging on by his or her fingernails, and what you did would change the course of that person's life forever, would that person get a smile or any expression of goodwill?

I heard someone ask another person, "Are you a Christian?" And the other person said, "Yes, of course I'm a Christian." To which the first person said pretty bluntly, "Then tell your face." Not everyone who is supposed to have the hope and joy of his or her faith puts it on display. In fact, some of us, from my observation, really know how to hide the joy and hope we claim to have with a perpetual frown or scowl. We could give a master class on how to look miserable. We have to intentionally remember sometimes that the attitude we wear on our face makes an impression.

This story of Kevin Hines demonstrates that we have an impact, and our impact may not require all that much from us. I have often heard it said that the average person will encounter roughly 10,000 people in a lifetime. These are not all best friends or people we know well. They are encounters, contacts, acquaintances, those we may meet once and never see again. For some of us, of course, it will be far less, as our living arrangement—say, as a farmer or one who works from home—is somewhat solitary in this respect. Others—traveling salesmen, for example, or ministers at large churches (my co-author had me put that one in)—will meet many times that number.

But on average, so they say, it is 10,000. Ten thousand! Pause here for a minute and think about that number.

Think of the impact we will have on other people and on the world. We don't have to be captains of industry or governors of states or quarterbacks in the NFL to encounter that many. Little old me and you are making that kind of an impact in our lifetimes and even on a daily basis.

There's a funny story that illustrates the way we can affect another person. A chief executive officer of a large company was traveling with his wife, and they stopped for gas. The CEO went inside and, when he came out, noticed his wife talking to the gas station attendant. As they drove off, he asked why she was talking to him. It turned out she knew the attendant and used to date him.

Feeling smug, he said, "I'll bet you're thinking you're glad you married me, a CEO, and not that gas station attendant." But she said, "No, I wasn't thinking that." So, he asked, "What were you thinking?" She replied, "Well, I was thinking that if I'd married him, he'd be the CEO and you'd be a gas station attendant."

I believe without question that every one of us is going to make an impact. Maybe not quite as dramatic as turning an ordinary man into a CEO, as this woman claimed she could, but we will make an impact. And not just on one other person, probably; we will have the opportunity to impact many, to make a small impact on the whole world. Even a chance encounter gives us the opportunity to make an impact of hope or an impact of discouragement—in the work we do, the people we meet, where we volunteer, our involvement at church, and in the community.

The only question is: What kind of an impact are we going to make?

Allow me to finish the story of Kevin Hines, at least up until 2019 when the CNN story ran. He and Sanjay Gupta walked back out to that spot where he had jumped, and Sanjay asked him how it felt to be at the place where he almost died. Kevin corrected him and said, "This is the place where I lived."

Something new was born in him during the following months and years, and his rebirthed life has caused him to travel all over the world on a mission to eradicate suicide. Advocating for the nets on the Golden Gate Bridge is but one of his endeavors. Through his public speaking, storytelling, and films, Kevin is regularly showing the compassion, kind words, and "friendly eyes" that no one had given him when he needed it most.

He would never claim this for himself, but those who know him best estimate that he has probably saved hundreds of lives along the way.

Can it be that we might begin to live more fully, that something great comes alive in us, when we share friendly eyes and more with other people? Can we find that time and place where we lived—where we made the decision to live— and where that decision encouraged and empowered us to help others to live. That decision can be made today, right now; we don't have to wait for some cataclysmic episode to take action.

We simply need to see that we can live more fully and help others live, believe in our impact, and then go forth with this new perspective and attitude.

The 75th anniversary of the D-Day landings at Normandy in June 1944, which began to free Europe from the tyranny of Nazi Germany during World War II, reminded me of a story. It was told to me by a World War II veteran who was not himself there on D-Day but heard it from a friend who was. This man lost his leg as he was landing on Omaha Beach, the scene of the highest casualties that day.

A memorial to the events of D-Day at Omaha Beach.

Of course, his wound ended the war for him, and he came home bitter about the loss of his leg. He never talked about it, but there always seemed to be this animosity and resentment just below the surface.

One year, he went back to Omaha Beach. He had not been there since the day he lost his leg, but it was during an anniversary celebration to which he'd been invited, so he decided to go. He walked around the national cemetery and along the beach, amazed that he and other young men could possibly have done what they were called on to do and that anyone had survived. At one point, a French woman who was strolling along saw him, figured out his rough age in her mind, and noticed his slight limp. She went up to him and asked, "Are you an American? Were you here?" He answered yes to both questions.

She threw her arms around him. "You saved me!" she said. "I was just a little girl, but I remember. You saved me and my family. We can never repay you except to say thank you." After the man returned home from that trip, he was never bitter again. He was willing to talk just a bit about his experiences during the war, too.

He would sometimes say, "Now I know for whom I gave my leg."

We toss around the word "hero" a lot these days, but certainly that word applies to this man and many like him who remain unnamed and unknown to us. There is simply something heroic about those who are asked and are willing to commit themselves, invest themselves, to save the lives and futures of other people.

To save a life is no small thing. You and I may never be called on to do it in the particular way of Kevin Hines or this soldier who landed on Omaha Beach. We truly need those who are willing to risk their lives, who run toward gunfire rather than away, who go into burning buildings when others are running out, so that others might be saved.

But even if we have not taken on that kind of responsibility, we can still be in the business of impacting other people, of helping, of even saving lives. It is no small thing to save a life, but we can do it in a variety of small ways.

A few years ago, the church I attend was part of a worldwide campaign to end malaria. It is a preventable and curable disease, spread mostly through infected mosquitoes, that hits the people of sub-Saharan Africa the hardest, especially the children. Since I give directly to a variety of individuals and causes that are important to me, I didn't necessarily perk up that much when the church offered one more thing to which I might contribute.

But then I heard that one of the important areas to be funded was the purchase of bed nets for children and families. For every $10 donated, an insecticide-treated bed net would be given to protect a child or adult as they slept at night. Ten dollars would save one life.

I thought to myself, "Ten dollars!" I don't know about you, but it's not that often that I am able to save a life for only $10. I suddenly found myself wanting to save not just one life, but ten or 100 or more!

That campaign has not been successful, as of the writing of this, in entirely ending malaria, nor does it look like we will anytime soon. But incredible progress has been made and lives have been saved. I know the statistic currently cited is that a child in Africa dies from malaria every two minutes, which is appalling, but the statistic before the campaign began was a death every 30 seconds.

If anything, this steels my determination to make an impact wherever I can, even if we can't completely wipe out all of the worst things that are wrong in our world. We have to keep looking around, keep seeing the opportunities that are there to save a life, and keep giving of ourselves to make it so. We have to keep trying!

Before my co-author became a minister, he had been a lawyer. The church he and his wife attended in New York City supported him through the transition. They hired him as the assistant minister and watched him grow into the role of preacher and pastor during his three years in seminary. Everyone thought it was so courageous and monumental for him to switch careers like this, but for him it was just what he felt he had to do, what he was called to do.

He would tell you it was the easiest decision he ever made.

A few years after he graduated and was ordained, he returned for a visit to that church that had been so nurturing to him during that time. He met a woman that day, one he could just barely remember. She told him that she had once been a lawyer too and that, since he'd been gone from the church, she had switched careers to be a teacher. "And," she said, "you are the one who gave me the courage to do it. I didn't think I could make such a drastic change, but I felt that if you could do it, so could I!"

He couldn't remember her name, had no idea she was even thinking about it, but he made an impact on her that totally transformed her vocation and her life. I tell him jokingly that it doesn't really count because he wasn't aware he was doing it, but in my opinion, he saved that woman's life. She had been unfulfilled before, going through the motions, putting in her time not just in her career but in her life. Now she is fully alive and engaged and loving it! That is what it means to save a life, isn't it?

Following his death in 2018, one of the many stories about former president George H. W. Bush that resurfaced was of the letter he left for Bill Clinton on the desk in the Oval Office on his first day as president. It was written after the contentious 1992 campaign that he had hoped to win but was now vacating the office to his rival instead. The letter said:

> *Dear Bill,*
>
> *When I walked into this office just now I felt the same sense of wonder and respect that I felt four years ago. I know you will feel that, too.*
>
> *I wish you great happiness here. I never felt the loneliness some Presidents have described.*
>
> *There will be very tough times, made even more difficult by criticism you may not think is fair. I'm not a very good one to give advice; but just don't let the critics discourage you or push you off course.*
>
> *You will be our President when you read this note. I wish you well. I wish your family well.*
>
> *Your success now is our country's success. I am rooting hard for you.*
> *Good luck –*
> *George*

Encouragement. To encourage someone else is the surest way I know to save that person's life. I have found that people are desperate for encouragement. I remember the story of a young man who was just starting out in the ministry and seeking some advice from his father, a seasoned pastor. He said, "Dad, I want to be an encourager in my ministry. I want to encourage people. Can you give me a few pointers on when I can tell if people really need to be encouraged?"

And his father said, "Son, if they are breathing, they need to be encouraged." I have never, like this man's father, come across a person who didn't need to be encouraged.

Another famous letter of encouragement is from John Wesley, the founder of the Methodist movement in the late eighteenth century, to William Wilberforce, a member of Parliament in Great Britain and strong advocate for the abolition of slavery. Six days before his death, Wesley's last known letter went to Wilberforce, who was in a desperate struggle against this great evil. In the pertinent part, he wrote:

> *Unless God has raised you up for this very thing, you will be worn out by the opposition of men and devils. But if God be for you, who can be against you? Are all of them together stronger than God? O be not weary of well-doing! Go on, in the name of God and in the power of his might, till even American*

slavery (the vilest that ever saw the sun) shall vanish away before it.

The once-impregnable fortress of slavery was already beginning to crumble. With Wilberforce's determination, a few years later, in 1807, the practice of buying and selling slaves was outlawed. Finally, shortly before his death in 1833, his lifelong quest was realized when the ownership of slaves was completely abolished in the United Kingdom. Within a few more decades, in 1863, slaves were emancipated in the United States.

William Wilberforce.

We all need to be encouraged. We all need to be inspired, to be lifted up, and to be told that we are being rooted for, that our lives are valuable, that they have meaning, that the work we are doing is important, that others support us, that God is with us. We all need to be driven to bigger and better ideals and goals.

Do you remember the famous and thrilling quote from Jack Nicholson in the movie *As Good as It Gets*? He can't quite get the words out at first, but he ends up paying his new friend, who he hopes will one day become his girlfriend, the supreme compliment: "You make me want to be a better man."

We have been talking about saving the life of another person. It is a tremendous gift to be the encourager of another, to motivate him or her to be a better, truer, greater person. I've found that a real leader will focus on what the other person can become, not necessarily on what that person is at this particular moment. Treat people as if they already are what they potentially might be, and they will often end up becoming that person.

The greatest gift you can give someone else is the gift of hope. Hope provides meaning and a future, no matter what the circumstances may be around us right at that moment. Therefore, resolve to give someone hope. Give everyone you meet hope in every situation you can. We probably wouldn't be where we are now if someone had not given us the gift of hope.

Take the initiative, be the thermostat, boldly plant little seeds of hope wherever you go. Robert Louis Stevenson, the writer of *Dr. Jekyll and Mr. Hyde* and *Treasure Island*, wrote, "Don't judge each day by the harvest you reap but by the seeds you plant."

I always found the story of the medieval monk who was watering his garden one morning both bewildering and energizing. A man was walking along and asked the monk, "Father, if you knew you were dying tonight, what would you do?" The monk thought a moment before replying: "These flowers would still need watering."

This story has always been bewildering, as I say, to me and to anyone I have told it to because it seems to go against the grain of our nature to do something that so obviously will not benefit us in any way. If I water on the very last day of my life, what am I going to get out of it? Isn't the whole point of one's life to get for yourself the most out of whatever you are doing?

The answer to that is "No." At least, not when you are thinking of the impact you can have. I think the real energy comes when you know that your work is for something larger than just yourself, something beyond you, something that will endure and inspire and affect others, maybe for generations to come. What I start, if it is truly worthwhile, may not be finished during my career, or even during my lifetime. There is satisfaction in knowing the impact I have begun will go on and on. The more monumental our dreams and achievements are, the more this is true. To create lasting value with one's life is the most significant thing one can do.

I've heard it said that the best time to plant a tree was 20 years ago, but the second-best time is right now. The principle here is the same. It would be great if the tree was already here, we'd have the shade and fruit to enjoy right now. But if someone didn't plant that tree back then, the only way there will ever be a tree here for me, or more likely for others, to enjoy is for me to put it in the ground now.

I am the one who is here. I am the one who sees the need. I am the one with the ability to plant the seed. It has come to depend on me to plant the seed that will make the impact that I see needs to be made, and I must decide if I will indeed make that impact.

I know of a man who by the time he was 19 and in college knew where he was headed and what he wanted out of life. Among other things, he wanted to make a ton of money. That is, until someone he trusted and respected pulled him aside one day and asked him this question that shook him to his foundations: "Bill, what are you doing with your life that will last forever?"

The question haunted him. He began to realize that his whole existence was wrapped up in the here and now. Everything he was doing was self-centered and temporary. He was spending his life pursuing material things that would one day all be gone. Stripped naked and vulnerable by the question, and trying to find

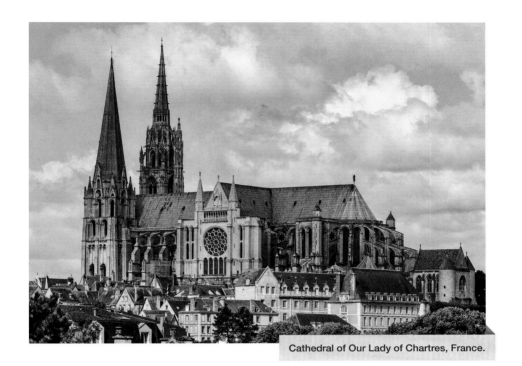

Cathedral of Our Lady of Chartres, France.

meaning in his existence, he made the decision to pour his life into other people, whose lives and souls would last forever.

What are you doing with your life that will last forever? I'm hoping this question will haunt you just a little bit, too, and shake you to your foundations. Truly deep and significant impact means that the desire for what I am doing primarily to benefit myself right now has to be outweighed by the desire for what I am doing to make a lasting difference. Providing hope, encouraging others, planting seeds that will flourish and grow, influencing people who will go on to influence others, giving your life away to ensure that someone else has the tools to create a life that has value—these are the surest ways I know for what you do to last forever.

A traveler is said to have come from Italy to the French town of Chartres to see the great cathedral being built there. Arriving at the end of the day, he went to the site just as the workmen were leaving for home. He asked one man, covered with dust, what he did there. The man replied that he was a stonemason. He spent his days carving rocks. Another man, when asked, said he was a glassblower who spent his days making slabs of colored glass. Still another workman replied that he was a blacksmith who pounded iron for a living.

Wandering into the deepening gloom of the unfinished edifice, the traveler came upon an older woman, armed with a broom, sweeping up the stone chips and wood shavings and glass shards from the day's work. "What are you doing?" he asked. The woman paused, leaning on her broom, and looking up toward the high arches, replied, "Me? I'm building a cathedral for the glory of God Almighty."

The workers at Chartres, especially perhaps this old woman who was merely cleaning up the remnants of the day, had a magnificent vision of what they were creating for the future. They began something they knew they would never see completed. They built for something larger and grander than just themselves.

I am reminded of the words of Abraham Lincoln near the beginning of the long, grinding conflict of the Civil War to keep the country united and make it free for everyone: "The struggle of today, is not altogether for today— it is for a vast future also." We must perceive what we do in the same way.

My favorite television commercial as I am writing this is, as usual, one that I am not quite sure exactly what it is advertising. A grandfather and grandmother have agreed to keep their granddaughter for her senior year in high school, while her father moves to accommodate a new job elsewhere. The grandfather especially becomes deeply attached to his granddaughter and participates in various stages of her life that year, but he also spends time combing through the newspaper looking to find that dream car he has always wanted.

In the final scene, perhaps as she is set to graduate and move away to college or once again be with her father, the grandfather takes her outside to show her a car he has just purchased. She seems to think he has purchased his dream car. But when she turns around, he holds up the keys and gives them to her.

She exclaims, "But Grandpa, what about your dream car?" And he says, "This is my dream now."

When we believe in our impact, we begin to help the dreams of others come true.

In 1968, a man by the name of Kent Keith, a sophomore at Harvard College, wrote a booklet for the high school student leaders he'd been working with on the how and why of making an impact and leading meaningful, lasting change. The challenge, he felt, was to do what is right and good and true and keep striving, no matter what. As part of this booklet, he came up with what he called "The Paradoxical Commandments":

People are illogical, unreasonable and self-centered. Love them anyway.

If you do good, people will accuse you of selfish ulterior motives. Do good anyway.

If you are successful, you will win false friends and true enemies. Succeed anyway.

The good you do today will be forgotten tomorrow. Do good anyway.

Honesty and frankness make you vulnerable. Be honest and frank anyway.

The biggest men and women with the biggest ideas can be shot down by the smallest men and women with the smallest minds. Think big anyway.

People favor underdogs but follow only top dogs. Fight for a few underdogs anyway.

What you spend years building may be destroyed overnight. Build anyway.

People really need help but may attack you if you do help them. Help people anyway.

Give the world the best you have and you'll get kicked in the teeth. Give the world the best you have anyway.

It's the rare person who can live up to these commandments because it involves continuing to build and fight and pursue and give regardless of what you are getting back. Nevertheless, I encourage you to try to be that rare person because sometimes what you get back when you live this way is a changed and liberated life. To have a ready smile and "friendly eyes," which is where we began this chapter, may even save someone who will go on to do great things.

I'm not sure if it helps to know that a list of the Paradoxical Commandments was found on the wall of the children's home in Calcutta that was run by Mother Teresa after her death. No one knows exactly how she learned of these, where she got them, or to what effect or purpose she used them. Kent Keith was absolutely stunned to hear of this, 30 years after he had written them, and thrilled to know someone he had long admired had been impacted in at least a small way by his own creative endeavor. Sometimes, that is the way it works.

What I have been trying to bring home to you in this book is how you can believe and then watch it come true. You can envision your future and then see it unfold, you can decide and then take steps toward your destiny. You can, in other words, set the thermostat of your life, not just passively be the thermometer, and have the attitude and purpose and goals you have set be what your life becomes. I have been encouraging you, in a sense, to find success at everything you set yourself to with your mind and heart and hands.

But I hope it has become clear—if not in previous chapters, then at least by now—that my true desire for you is that you will find more than mere success at what you put your hand to, that you will discover significance with your life. Baseball legend Jackie Robinson was quoted as saying, "A life isn't significant except for its impact on other lives."

My desire is that you will be inspired to have a reach with your life, an influence, an effect. I pray you will see the value of pouring vision and resilience and purpose and hope from your life into the lives of others, not for any selfish reason, but simply to realize the positive difference you can have on another person and on the world.

Jesus puts it in terms of blessing. He went everywhere speaking words of blessing and encouraging people to bless others. Now, blessing can mean happiness or contentment or peacefulness. But perhaps the best definition for this word from Jesus' time is to "find the right path" or "find the right direction." Your impact can help others find the right direction for themselves.

Part of the process of blessing is to treat someone as he or she might become and then watch as he or she grows into that person. It is treating other people as if they have already arrived at the place where you envision them to be some day and then seeing them reach that destination. Jesus is our model for doing this; he was the master at it. But you and I can be good at it, too.

Remember my prayer from Chapter Six? I encourage you, as you put all of the elements of this book to work in your own life—as you speak positive and productive words to yourself, as you envision what your life might be, as you take action now, as you overcome obstacles and opposition, as you discover your purpose, as you ask God to empower you, as you come to terms with your past, as you are emboldened for the future, and as you work collaboratively with others; as you boldly become the thermostat for yourself and those around you, in other words—that you pull it all together each day with this prayer: "Oh Lord, I'm not looking for blessings to come into my life, I'm looking to be a blessing. Please make me a blessing."

I am convinced you will find the right path for yourself and others and will be a person of true significance.

John Phillip Newell is a Scottish preacher who now lives in the United States and writes books and leads seminars. He tells about his father, who was also a minister and who always liked a certain blessing from the Bible:

> The Lord bless you and keep you.
> The Lord make his face to shine upon you and be gracious unto you.

The Lord lift up the light of his countenance upon you
And give you his peace.

He always liked that prayer, and in his later, declining years, he would use that prayer to bless people. Even when he couldn't find the words for other things because of some dementia that was setting in, when he said that prayer, the words would just flow. At the nursing home where he lived, after dinner, he would say, "I have to go and bless the people now," and he would go from table to table and say this prayer. The words would flow and his face would shine, and the faces of all the people would be shining.

At one point, Newell had to go with his father to sell his car after he could no longer drive. There was a young car salesman who helped them and was very kind and gracious to his father during this delicate task. At the end of the transaction, when they were all standing and shaking hands, Newell said to this young salesman, "I think my father would like to bless you now as we end."

The young man agreed to this, although I'm not sure that he knew what was happening. Newell's father took his hands and looked in his face and said, "The Lord bless you and keep you. The Lord make his face to shine upon you and be gracious unto you. The Lord lift up the light of his countenance upon you and give you his peace."

It was a moving moment. Newell looked up and tears were just streaming down this young man's face. And Newell thought, "This young man will never forget this moment, never."

And then he thought, "What if I could be the bearer of such blessing?" What if you and I could be the bearers of blessing and lasting impact and true significance that touches our families and communities and world?

STEP TEN

As objectively as you can, evaluate the attitude and demeanor you exhibit naturally to other people. Is it positive or negative? Make the decision to change your disposition to one that is warmer and more approachable. See others as those who need hope and encouragement and see yourself as one who has been given the opportunity to provide it. On what one person could you make the greatest lasting, positive impact? Decide to pour your time and best qualities into that person. Pray the prayer, "Oh Lord, I'm not looking for blessings to come into my life, I'm looking to be a blessing. Please make me a blessing," each day for a week and see what happens.

ABOUT THE AUTHORS

Dr. Kevin Elko is a nationally renowned sports psychologist, performance and career-enhancement consultant, author, and professional motivational speaker.

In sports, he has consulted with various successful NFL teams including the Pittsburgh Steelers, the Dallas Cowboys, the Philadelphia Eagles, the Miami Dolphins, and the New Orleans Saints. In college athletics, he has worked with seven BCS National Championship football teams including University of Miami, LSU, University of Alabama, and Florida State University.

In the business world, Dr. Elko focuses on helping organizations in the areas of leadership, goal setting, and motivation. His corporate clients have included ING, Tyson Foods, Abbott Labs, LPL Financial, The Hartford, Genworth, Jackson National Life, Pioneer Investments, Morgan Stanley, Bank of America, Merrill Lynch, and Sun Life, among others.

Dr. Elko is the author of several books: *The Sender: A Story About When Right Words Make All the Difference*, *Nerves of Steel*, *The Pep Talk*, *True Greatness: Mastering the Inner Game of Business Success*, and *Touchdown: Achieving Your Greatness on the Playing Field of Business and Life*.

He received his bachelor's degree in biology education and coaching from California University of Pennsylvania. He received two master's degrees and a doctorate at West Virginia University and was later inducted into West Virginia University Hall of Fame.

"To Joye, Steve, Lou Ann and Shawn—my Christian Family. You four have been a mighty cloud of witness to the power of faith—I love you all more than you know."

Duane Thompson is passionate about giving people hope and equipping them to believe they can set a new direction for their lives. He is a lawyer and ordained minister. After having practiced at a large, international law firm on Wall Street and served as senior pastor at a 3,500-member congregation in the suburbs of Pittsburgh, Duane is currently the senior pastor of Southport United Methodist Church in Indianapolis. He is a graduate of George Washington University National Law Center in Washington, D.C., and Union Theological Seminary in New York City.

"This book is dedicated to Brenda—my wife, companion and inspiration."

IMAGE CREDITS

Foreword: Pg viii–ix, Library of Congress.

Introduction: Pg 1, Stuart Monk / Shutterstock. Pg 3, Kevin Kelley and Sheldon Smith. Pg 5, World Economic Forum, Photo by Monica Flueckiger / Shutterstock. Pg 6: Philip Lange / Shutterstock.

Chapter 1: Pg 8–9: Oliver Le Moal / Shutterstock. Pg 11: Dirk Ercken / Shutterstock. Pg 14: Andrey_Popov / Shutterstock. Pg 22: Serg64/Shutterstock.

Chapter 2: Pg 24–25: Petr Toman / Shutterstock. Pg 26: hxdbzxy/Shutterstock. Pg 28: Barry Salmons / Shutterstock. Pg 29: Leonard Zhukovsky / Shutterstock.

Chapter 3: Pg 40–41: Bishonen / Wikimedia Commons. Pg 46: Library of Congress. Pg 50: Kathy Hutchins / Shutterstock. Pg 54: Airman 1st Class Christopher Williams / Wikimedia Commons.

Chapter 4: Pg 56–57: JK Multimedia / Shutterstock. Pg 59: KKulikov/Shutterstock. Pg 63: Wikimedia Commons. Pg 65: Library of Congress. Pg 70: Debby Wong / Shutterstock.

Chapter 5: Pg 72–73: Ken Drysdale / Shutterstock. Pg 79: Brad Bywater / Shutterstock. Pg 81: Wikimedia Commons. Pg 83: Fernando Cortes / Shutterstock. Pg 84: Francisco Javier Diaz / Shutterstock.

Chapter 6: Pg 88–89: Photo Junction / Shutterstock. Pg 92: Kim Traynor / Wikimedia Commons. Pg 94: Everett Historical / Shutterstock. Pg 98: Everett Historical / Shutterstock. Pg 100: BLFootage / Shutterstock.

Chapter 7: Pg 104–105, David Lee / Shutterstock. Pg 107, The Grable Group. Pg 108, Hayk_Shalunts / Shutterstock. Pg 115, Wikimedia Commons. Pg 117, Nicku/Shutterstock. Pg 119, David Hume Kennerly / Wikimedia Commons. Pg 120, Krista Kennell / Shutterstock.

Chapter 8: Pg 122–123, Library of Congress. Pg 125, BasPhoto / Shutterstock. Pg 126–127, Library of Congress. Pg 128, AzriSuratmin / Shutterstock. Pg 129, Adam Jones / Wikimedia Commons. Pg 130, Margaret Suckley, FDR Presidential Library & Museum / Wikimedia Commons. Pg 135, PeterVrabel / Shutterstock.

Chapter 9: Pg 140–141, New York Public Library. Pg 143, Henk Lindeboom, from the Dutch National Archives / Wikimedia Commons. Pg 145, Katie Rommel-Esham / Wikimedia Commons. Pg 150, Gina Smith / Shutterstock. Pg 151, Myotis/Shutterstock. Pg 152, Debby Wong / Shutterstock.

Chapter 10: Pg 158–159, dibrova/Shutterstock. Pg 160, U.S. Army Corps of Engineers Sacramento District / Wikimedia Commons. Pg 163, Alessandro Colle / Shutterstock. Pg 167, Morphart Creation / Shutterstock. Pg 169, Radu Razvan / Shutterstock.

INDEX